The Rt Revd Nick Baines, is the Bishop of Leeds. Previously he was the Bishop of Bradford and, prior to that, the Bishop of Croydon.

He read German and French at Bradford University and, before ordination, worked for four years as a Russian linguist at GCHQ.

Indeed, Nick's particular expertise lies in communication. He has nearly 15,000 followers on Twitter and his blog has been viewed more than 2 million times. He is regularly heard on Radio 2 and Radio 4, is often asked to comment nationally on topical issues and has written seven books on Christian faith.

Nick has been a member of the House of Lords since 2014, leading on Europe, Russia, Sudan, security and intelligence. He has represented the Archbishop of Canterbury at international faith conferences and, for 11 years, was the English Co-chair of the Meissen Commission, which develops relationships between the Church of England and the EKD (Protestant Church in Germany). Preaching frequently in Germany – in German – Nick also has a keen interest in music, literature, art, film, theatre and Liverpool FC. He's married to Linda (a health visitor and artist) and they have three adult children and three grandchildren.

FREEDOM IS COMING

From Advent to Epiphany with the
prophet Isaiah

Nick Baines

First published in Great Britain in 2019

Society for Promoting Christian Knowledge
36 Causton Street
London SW1P 4ST
www.spck.org.uk

British Library Cataloguing-in-Publication Data
A catalogue record for this book is available from the British Library

ISBN 978–0–281–08291–9
eBook ISBN 978–0–281–08292–6

1 3 5 7 9 10 8 6 4 2

Typeset by Manila Typesetting Company
First printed in Great Britain by Jellyfish Print Solutions
Subsequently digitally reprinted in Great Britain

eBook by Manila Typesetting Company

Produced on paper from sustainable forests

Contents

Contents

Introduction

There is nothing new under the sun. That's what a poet wrote nearly three thousand years ago in the Middle East. Maybe it was the relentless struggle to survive in a hot climate in an area dominated by desert. Perhaps he was caught in one of those moments of realization when the roll of one day into another suddenly seems endless and inherently somewhat pointless. Nothing ever changes. We are born, we live, we die – and that's the end of the matter.

This poet would not be the first to experience this or to consider if human life is essentially pointless and he isn't the last. Literature is littered with examples of people asking fundamental questions about life, meaning, ethics, history and death. Sometimes, whole nations or communities find themselves compelled to address these fundamental questions in circumstances they would never have chosen and amid experiences they would prefer not to have had.

We could find illustrations of this in any generation. For example, within living memory, how did the Christian Church handle the dehumanizing brutality of Nazism in the 1930s and 1940s when theology could no longer remain a matter of personal piety or 'mere spirituality', but demanded an informed and courageous – prophetic, even – response to social change? Alternatively, more relevant to us in the twenty-first century, how are people to respond when – to quote the constant lament of the psalmists – 'the rich prosper and the poor are sent empty away'?

The world is not a comfortable place just now. As someone once remarked in relation to postmodernism, 'We know what it is post, but we don't know what it is pre.' So, we find ourselves – as individuals, as societies and as nations – towards the end of the second decade of the twenty-first century, having to think again about who we are, why we are the way we are, where we have failed and what really matters.

1

Christians face a further challenge: if we are called to be faithful to the call of God in whatever generation, how do we know that we are being faithful and not simply shaping God in our own image?

These are not new questions. Every generation asks them in some way or other. But it takes courage, humility and repentance (a willingness to change our minds – to be conformed to the will of God, however uncomfortable or inconvenient that might prove to be) to address this reality . . . and no one finds that an easy task.

To help us, however, we might choose to dig deeper into the wisdom of the ancients and take a longer look at why they found themselves in a place of profound questioning and serious challenge. What can we learn from them? In the light of their experiences, successes and failures, what happens when, uninvited, our world changes radically and all the certainties dissolve before our eyes? Which voices do we listen to when, in an age of seemingly infinite communications media, we feel we might drown under the deluge of contradictory appeals for attention or obeisance? How do we know that our 'vision' is the right one when the evidence of our eyes challenges this view every moment of every day? In the words of the Old Testament theologian Walter Brueggemann (1997), how do we hear the 'cadences of home' amid the strange rhythms and melodies of an alien people?

These are precisely the questions being asked by the people who populate the pages and stories of the Old Testament. It could be argued that the poets, historians and writers who contributed to what we call 'Scripture' did not know they were writing holy literature; they had their own purposes in mind and their own audiences in sight. They recorded their narratives and stated their cases in answer to some fundamental questions of identity: who are we, why are we here, why are things the way they are, how did we come to be where we are, what is the point of it all, where will it all end up, why bother?

These are the questions being addressed by the poets who wrote what we know as Genesis 1—11. Rather than asking *how* the world came into being, they are actually trying to account for *why* the world is the way it is. In these texts we hear those haunting words of God, walking in the garden in the cool of the day and asking an embarrassed Adam and Eve that question from which human beings have never been able to escape: 'Mortal being, where are you?' Knowing now that they are transparent – 'naked', seen through – they have followed their instinct to hide, only to discover two facts of life: (a) that there is no hiding place and (b) being found need not be something to be feared but, instead, something to be prized.

These are also questions asked by the people of Jesus' time in Ancient Israel. The holy God cannot be present alongside – or contaminated by collocation with – the unholy, pagan Roman imperial occupying forces, so how do we worship and serve a God who seems impotent in the face of generations of superpower subjugation? How should we remain faithful to our inherited identity and vocation when every day seems to reinforce our stupidity or, as modern atheists might term it, credulity? And for how long should we even try to remain faithful when taunted by our conquerors for our apparent stubborn denial of 'reality'?

Maybe the people of Jesus' time handled this by reaching back into the story that shaped their self-understanding. Called to live and give their lives in order to show the world who God is and what God is about, they had gradually lost the plot. Literally: they had forgotten who and what they had been called to be and then, consequently, had been exiled from the land that was the earthed token of God's covenant of relationship with them. They got caught up in all the fantasies that grow out of hubris, revenge, power, security and insular complacency. A people who told stories and celebrated festivals about their liberation by God successively failed to learn that this experience (to say nothing of this theological understanding of their identity and purpose) was supposed to shape their way of living in the world. For example, to sing songs of justice while enshrining injustices in their social order was to live hypocritically – a denial of the very reason for their existence.

One part of the Hebrew Scriptures that illustrates this comes in the middle of the words of one of the most prominent prophets of the eighth century before Christ – probably the time and context in which the creation narratives of Genesis 1—11 were originally composed. Nothing is ever addressed to a vacuum and prophecies relate to real time, space, place, politics and people. Isaiah lived through four kings of Judah and a host of political changes. The book (or three books, as we shall see later) covers a period from the eighth to the sixth century before Christ and its heart beats around a simple message: trust in Yahweh, not in political or military alliances that promise much and are always short-term expedients.

Isaiah speaks to a people who do not want to hear bad news; they think they are invincible, that their God can be taken for granted as being on their side and 'good news' is that which speaks of a glorious future for them. Right at the beginning of his book, Isaiah exposes this bizarre situation, using image and sarcasm to strip back the veneer of respectable religion and to see through the pretended theologies of self-fulfilment and self-satisfaction. He pulls no punches and takes no prisoners: you have lost the plot and the consequences of not recovering it will be dire.

And here it gets really interesting.

The prophets are not people who have some sort of magic insight into the future. They are not mere gifted charismatics who receive special insight from God, allowing them to see what others cannot perceive and to hear messages to which others are deaf. Rather, they seem to be people who have done their homework. They have studied not only their Scriptures – the stories and narratives that shaped their experience and understanding of God, the world and themselves – but also economics, politics, history, literature and philosophy. In different ways and from different backgrounds, they have dug into the ways of the world and the motivations of 'powers' and people, and tried to look at past, present and future through a different lens. They have shone a unique and consistent light on to familiar realities and drawn conclusions from what they have observed that are unusually clear and clearly were unpopular. They had the courage to look truth in the eye and not to be seduced by easier visions.

The book of Isaiah is really three books, or one book in three parts. Chapters 1—39 are comprised of a variety of approaches to alerting people to the problem: you have lost your way as God's people with a unique human vocation in God's world and, if you don't recover this vocation, you will lose everything that speaks to you of who you are, how God sees you, where your future lies, even why you matter in the first place. 'Get real' might be the most concise contemporary way to summarize Isaiah's message.

Chapters 40—55 are addressed to those people who, as it turned out, had chosen not to heed Isaiah's warnings. They have now lost everything and find themselves exiled by the neighbouring empire whose mockery is hard to bear. Every day they wake up, they see apparent evidence of their own credulity and the misguided fantasy of their disappointed faith. To quote a poet of the time, 'How can we sing the Lord's song in a strange land?' In other words, how can we sing songs about God, the Creator and Sustainer of all that is, when we have now been sitting for several generations by the riverbanks of our pagan enemies, who mock our weakness by taunting us to sing our unreal songs? Or, to put it more pointedly, how can we keep believing in God when all the evidence points to him either (a) not being there at all or (b) not being as strong as other people's mere tribal deities?

These are hard questions and they are not merely theoretical. Faith has never been a simple matter of private opinion, but is always inextricably tied up with ethics, politics, economics and the pragmatism of everyday life. Isaiah's remit is to expose the reality, reject illusion and demand responsibility. Blaming God or other people is not enough; when all is stripped away, we must begin our critical questioning with ourselves and our own accountability.

This sort of honesty requires courage and some sense that the future is still open. It calls from a beleaguered people a willingness to have their curiosity awakened and their imagination teased by the hint of a possibility that things can change and the world be transformed. In other words, it calls for hope. That is, not some sort of optimism or wishful thinking that things will somehow get better, but a vision that sees through present pretensions and holds on to something worth living and dying for. This is about capturing the imagination and will of a people whose world has fallen apart, whose disappointment threatens to overwhelm and who can only reshape the world if they face reality, are grasped by hope and take responsibility for making change happen.

If they can't change their circumstances in the short term, at least they can change their disposition in the immediate present, learning from the past and directing their behaviour into and for the future.

In one sense, what prophets such as Isaiah call for is the daring audacity to try to look through God's eyes at the world and oneself. It is the nerve to expand one's vision, to broaden its scope and fill it with surprising colour and perspective. It is a way of being and seeing that dispenses with fear and embraces the future, regardless of what it might bring.

To complete the picture of Isaiah's narrative, chapters 56—66 see the people, after the exile has ended and the prophet's words of promise seem to have come true, wrestling with how now to live and work and worship in the light of their experiences. Again, their view is long and their vision broad. They have learned, through exile and a fundamental re-examination of themselves and their priorities, that today has to be understood and lived out in the context of tomorrow and eternity. In other words, their vision has to be one that transcends the immediate and shines light back from the future on to today, putting today's perceptions, attractions and urgencies into a critical perspective.

Advent is that 'waiting time' when Christians make space to remember the story of God's people waiting for God to come among them again. We put back together the elements of the story that led to

Jesus of Nazareth and the eventual changing of the world. In doing so, we recognize that the story does not begin with Jesus himself but is rooted in creation, the call of God's people, the voices of the prophets, and the developing experience of God's people and those with whom they come into contact. What is sometimes called 'the Jesus event' will make sense only when we have taken the time and space to listen afresh to the story that leads to (and, indeed, from) him.

So, Advent offers us not only the opportunity to learn about Old Testament prophets and what bugged them but also to examine ourselves and what shapes our seeing and listening and thinking. It gives us time and space to think seriously about what sort of God is drawing us towards Christmas and what sort of Messiah we will find acceptable. In engaging with this exercise, we might also face the truth that we are called to be committed agents of hope, not mere observers of other idols.

Week 1: Hearing voices

WEEK 1: SUNDAY

Introduction to the week

As we enter into the experience of the exiled people to whom the prophet Isaiah addresses his words, we are going to be using not only our minds but also our imaginations. We need to try to enter into the experience of people who have lived so long in a place where God seems to be absent that they find it hard to hear words of hope. There are also those who have settled into the new arrangement in Babylon and don't now want to be disturbed. All will be confronted by the call of God to move on in faith to a new place.

It is not a huge stretch for us to reflect on our own experience in the light of our imaginative investment in the predicament of the exiles – not only as individuals but also as communities of Christians whose experiences might sometimes seem familiar. In preparation for the week ahead and the reflections on our Advent journey with Isaiah, we might make the space today to be quiet, to resist the temptation to 'do stuff' and, in the silence, open our minds to hear afresh the word of the Lord.

Of course, hearing the word of the Lord is not always as straightforward as we would like it to be. A little girl heard, 'I will make you fishers of men' as 'I will make you vicious old men' – an error that might have unfortunate consequences. So, in listening for the word of the Lord, we have to pay attention to checking what we think we hear against the record of Scripture and the experience of those who have gone before us.

WEEK 1: MONDAY

Living in exile (40.3)

In the wilderness prepare the way of the LORD.

Georg Friedrich Handel has offered generations of people a way into Old Testament prophecy. His famous *Messiah*, performed by choirs everywhere during Advent, provides people otherwise unfamiliar with the biblical text with a vocabulary for hope. Yet the haunting beauty of the music, with its rousing climax of the 'Hallelujah Chorus', does not make immediately accessible the powerful story its text shapes. (And why should it? Why should everything be easily accessible without some effort and bother to pursue it?)

The opening words of this second part of Isaiah – 'Comfort, O comfort my people, says your God' (40.1) – are addressed to a people who find notions of comfort difficult to entertain. They have been exiled from their homeland – the land that gave them not only a place to belong but also an identity as God's people. Removal from that land spoke loudly to them of more than mere geographical dislocation. Their exile cut them to the heart. Every day they woke up to look at Babylon's rivers and hear the mocking of their conquerors reminding them of their hopelessness – of their defeat and failure. Reality raised questions for them about God, their own identity and, probably for some, if they had been conned in the first place. To put it bluntly: did their present predicament signify either that (a) God had abandoned them or (b) God was, after all, just another tribal deity and, sadly, he was weaker than the gods of the Babylonians?

There is a backstory. The vocation of Israel as God's people had always been one of self-giving, of living together in the world in such a way as to demonstrate who God is and what God is about. The many instructions given to the people in their early days as a nation were not simply commandments for keeping them miserable. The

Ten Commandments themselves, delivered to a people in the desert who had forgotten their story, were designed to shape a society of what today might be called 'mutual flourishing'. Freedom and obligation belonged together; the individual found identity, meaning and place within the company of those who took seriously the demands of the common good.

At the heart of this way of ordering society was the matter of justice. More than just a word or a nice nebulous concept, 'justice' described the proper ordering of relationships in community under God. It assumed humility as well as adventure – culture and creativity as well as generosity. For example, we read in the book of Deuteronomy of the institution of rituals that involved memory, symbolism, action and cost. In chapter 26, the 'Festival of the First Fruits' involved bringing the first percentage (not the fag end) of your harvested crop to the priest; you then recited a creed, one that reminded you and your fellows that your ancestors had been nomads and all transient, material things come from God. Elsewhere they were required to leave crops at the edges of fields so that homeless and migrant people could always find something to eat.

The demand for justice, therefore, lies at the heart and origin of the vocation of God's people. It is not an afterthought, introduced anachronistically by later socialists; the promise of flourishing was always contingent on the exercising of mutual responsibility and generosity. The denial of justice would not go unnoticed by the God who had called his people in the first place. The prophets of the Old Testament find themselves compelled to confront this people with the fact that they had lost the plot – the narrative that gave them meaning and identity. *If you forget that you were once slaves, it won't be long before you start treating other people like slaves. Once you build your property empires, you will quickly forget that there was a time when you had nothing and could not save yourselves.*

To cut a long story short, the warnings of the prophets went unheeded in both the eighth and sixth centuries before Christ – and the

11

result was exile. Removal from their land was tantamount to removal from their God and all he had promised. That is where we pick up the story in Isaiah 40—55, at the point at which the people have been in exile for more than a generation.

So, remember that this exile did not just happen and then get quickly resolved. For many of these people it went on for decades. That meant they, their children and grandchildren grew up in an alien place. The children grew up not knowing any other reality. For them this was 'life as we know it' – normality. Yet their elders would insist on them speaking the language of home; would keep alive the songs of a different world; would try to believe in a different way of seeing the world and history, despite the evidence of their eyes and ears.

Now, that might sound weird to those familiar only with being at home in their native homeland. But to anyone living in a place that is not their 'home', the challenges will sound very familiar and, as we shall see later, they will be called to prepare the way of the Lord even when the evidence suggests he has abandoned them in a desert.

Lord God, help us not to forget our calling to live justly for the sake of your world. Amen.

WEEK 1: TUESDAY

Living in hope (40.5)

The glory of the LORD shall be revealed.

I have only once preached before the Queen and some of her family – at Sandringham several years ago. The lectionary readings for the day included Isaiah 42, so I decided to start with that. The parish where I was then living was 70 per cent ethnic Muslim;

the neighbouring parish over 80 per cent – statistics that surprised some in the congregation, not least as they raised questions about what it means to be an Anglican parish church in such a context. But the point was that, for those who had been born in this place, this was no longer 'home' – it had changed complexion and no longer reflected the Cornflakes image of England from the 1950s. Yet, for those who now live here (mostly first-, second-, third- and fourth-generation immigrants from Pakistan and India), it was also not 'home'. Home for the former was a romantic memory of a culture that existed only in the past; for the latter, home was both here *and* the place of their origin – in the same way that Brits living in Spain or the USA still jealously guard their native identity and have an ambiguous relationship with both their present and past domiciles.

At Sandringham, I began with this observation simply in order to help us open our imagination to the text of Isaiah 42 by first thinking about what it actually feels like to be displaced or 'homeless' – even when the displacement is by choice and not just circumstances shaped by others. Do we belong or not? How do we negotiate the daily round of life and work and family and society, creating an identity and a future while feeling that we are not at home – possibly not wanted or liked? What if we suspect that the natives feel we are the reason for their problems also?

In our own time, Syrian refugees have remarked that they have to deal with not only their internal traumatic feelings but also the prejudices and erroneous assumptions of their new hosts. One Syrian refugee in the Netherlands said, 'I had to leave everything behind, all those things I studied and worked so hard for for so many years. Here, we have to start from scratch in a foreign country with a foreign culture and a foreign language. I feel completely uprooted.' Another, having described the loss of everything he had owned (and the death of his fiancée in the civil war), concluded, 'Is it even possible to comprehend this kind of loss, if you haven't been through it yourself?' This reminds me of those Russian émigrés I met in Israel

20 years ago who felt they were treated as 'Jews' in Russia, only then to find themselves regarded as 'Russians' in Israel – still 'the others'.

To be exiled is to find a world has ended – that the new world involves a total dislocation. If we can imaginatively comprehend the nature of this sort of experience, then we are beginning to understand something of the life and mindset of those in exile to whom words of comfort are now to be spoken.

Yet dig imaginatively a little deeper into the experience of Isaiah's exiles and now ask how you might hear words of hope. What might sound hope-full? That your conquerors have decided to make space and learn from you, rather than just oppress or marginalize you? That exile is coming to an end? That your conqueror is about to face his own defeat and humiliation? That you and your family are all going to return to where your ancestors came from originally? Something else?

Think a little deeper about what the reality of this might actually imply. The distant past from which your parents or grandparents came no longer exists. Life, as we well know, moves on and everything changes. (I have lived in many parts of England, Germany and France, yet still feel cross when I return to a town after 20 years and find they have changed the one-way system or built houses on a beloved bit of countryside.) Your previous home will no longer be the home of your memory and your arrival back into it might be experienced by those now living there as an intrusion into their current reality. An outsider now, you might well still be an outsider in the place you have always thought of as 'home'. What do you take with you and what must (or should) you leave behind? What if your children don't want to go, given that they have only ever known 'exile' as home? How will you cope with the reality of home when the romanticized utopian fantasies prove to be disappointingly inappropriate?

You can see the problem. It is easy to speak glibly about the Jewish exiles of Isaiah's time hearing good news of comfort without thinking through the real experience of those involved. What would 'comfort' have sounded like to those people?

When Isaiah confidently states that the 'glory of the LORD shall be revealed' – still in the future – he is asking this depressed people to trust in something that looks impossible. It defies reality and all the evidence. The prophet, however, is seeking to awaken hope. Not wishful thinking or mere optimism, but hope. That hope will be focused on the person of God, not on circumstances or some formula to make them feel better about life and their lot.

> God of justice and mercy, look kindly on refugees and those in exile from home – and do this through those who claim to bear your name. Amen.

WEEK 1: WEDNESDAY

The longer view (40.4)

Every valley shall be lifted up.

At this juncture, we need to make a wider point. It can be put as bluntly as this: God's people have always been called to defy 'reality' by taking a longer view and looking at the world (and our experience of it) through different eyes. We can illustrate this by a quite cursory look through the Bible itself.

In Genesis, after Adam and Eve have given in to the temptation all of us give in to (to make it all about 'me'), they know that they are seen through. Nevertheless, they try to hide. It is God who comes looking for them in the garden in the cool of the day and asks where they are and what they think they are doing. In one sense, God is asking them to look beyond their 'nakedness' and to see 'being seen through' as something hopeful rather than punishing. They need not hide because they cannot hide – or, if they so choose, they can carry on pretending, living with their illusions. Yet the invitation is to see beyond their present embarrassment to a way of living that is un-afraid of transparency.

The prophets themselves, by various means, language and images, invite their people to see beyond the immediate – looking through God's eyes at who they are and where they are heading. Some polit-ical and military alliances looked to offer short-term security for the nation, but the prophets took a longer-term view and spelled out the potential implications. They were accused of what today might be termed 'Project Fear' (in Brexit parlance), but they were simply spell-ing out the potential consequences of decisions being made for the wrong reasons. (It is worth noting that even reluctant-but-faithful prophets such as Jeremiah were not spared the fate of their obdur-ate compatriots when exile ensued: as the prophet repeatedly makes clear and as we shall see later, faithfulness to God and his call does not offer an exemption from collective responsibility.)

Leap ahead and Jesus begins his public ministry with the same call: look differently at God, the world and yourselves, and refuse to be defined – or constrained – by your current circumstances or experience. For me, the clearest pointer to this is found in Mark's Gospel (1.14–15). Here, Jesus' message is summed up in four phrases: (a) the time is fulfilled; (b) the kingdom of God has come near; (c) re-pent; and (d) believe in the good news.

To a first-century Jew, essentially 'good news' would mean the Ro-mans leaving and us getting our land, worship and identity back. So, if now is the time – the Kairos, the appointed time – then why are the Romans still here and in charge? The evidence of our eyes and ears tells us that now cannot be the time of God's coming among us again. How can the Holy One be here while the blaspheming pagans are still here – the Holy cannot cohabit with the unclean? But here comes the challenge: 'repent' means literally 'change your mind' or, in this context, change the way you look at/for God in the world . . .

in order to change the way you see God, the world and us . . . in order to change the way you think about God, the world and us . . . in order to change the way you live in the world with God and us.

The rest of the Gospel is an account of who could (or would) 'repent' and who could (or would) not.

You can see the point here. Jesus dares people to consider the radical possibility that God can be here *even while the Romans remain* in charge of their immediate life and destiny. Might it be possible that God is less concerned about being contaminated by pagan uncleanness than he is about contaminating the world with grace and mercy and sacrificial love? What if God were to have broken out of the expectations in which you have thus far trapped him and might challenge the world as we know it? What if this is how God, despite our best endeavours to imprison him in a cage of our own expectations or preferences, actually is?

'Believe in the good news' is an invitation to those who dare to 'repent' so as to commit themselves now to live and speak and choose as if God's kingdom (presence) were already here – in defiance of apparent Roman domination.

Later in the New Testament we find the apostle Paul driving the same line to both Jewish and Gentile Christians across Asia, Europe and the Middle East. Rather than wait for the new messianic age to follow the current Roman age, he says, live now as a new community that believes the new age has already begun – in the life, crucifixion and resurrection of Jesus of Nazareth. God is doing something new in Jesus, so start living accordingly. The struggle to be grasped by this good news is what lies behind the story of the first Christian communities and provides the rationale for the letters written to them by the apostles.

In other words – and to return to the situation facing the exiles in Isaiah 40—55 – God's people are called to live in defiance of the 'reality' that the dominant powers think is both obvious and ultimate.

It might seem as if God is absent and uninterested in the fate of his people. Everyday experience might suggest that either God has fallen asleep or we have been conned. As Jesus would ultimately suggest through an empty tomb, however, violence, despair, destruction and death do not and will not have the final word in this world. And God's people, those who have had their imaginations, their hearts and their minds teased and grasped by a hope that draws them, might look ridiculous to those who are driven by fear, but they will still march to a different beat and dance to a different tune.

God's people are invited – dared, even – to look beyond 'now' to a time when what looks unlikely might actually happen, when every valley shall be lifted up and the desert will become fertile and fruitful.

God, who teases our imagination, inspire us to look through your eyes and not be driven by fear. Amen.

WEEK 1: THURSDAY

Comfort? (40.1)

Comfort, O comfort my people.

To a modern ear, the opening words of Isaiah's second book sound somewhat encouraging and gentle. Comfort is what we would all like, but what is meant here? Is comfort all about being protected, cushioned from the nasty stuff of life? Is it about not having any problems or inconveniences? Is it about something else?

The Bayeux Tapestry depicts the story of William the Conqueror's invasion of England in 1066. In one panel you can spot a bishop 'encouraging' a group of reluctant soldiers with the flat of his sword. The caption says this: 'Bishop Odo comforts the troops.' It seems that the Normans were both impressed and frightened by the fighting of the English troops under the command of King Harold. Some thought of deserting, others of simply refusing to go into battle, and that is when the good bishop came and comforted them. (They fought, Harold was killed, the English were defeated and the rest is history.)

Clearly, Bishop Odo didn't pat the fearful soldiers on the head and wish them well. Nor did he pretend life was easy or that all would turn out well. He didn't indulge in simplistic slogans or wishful thinking. It appears that he stood with the troops, led by example, faced with them the harsh and dangerous reality of battle and bloodshed. His 'comfort' must have been to strengthen their resolve, put the cost of their commitment into perspective and stop them running away – for the greater good and not just their individual preservation.

'Comfort', then, is not a soft word. It faces harsh reality head on and refuses to resort to illusion or fantasy. Isaiah, I suspect, uses the word 'comfort' as a strong, substantial, 'gird up your loins and get stuck in' exhortation to people: get a grip, steel your back, change is coming and it will (as always) be costly as well as rewarding. (A similar idea is found in Mark 10 when Jesus sends his friends to get Bartimaeus and bring him over. They offer the blind man the most wonderful invitation ever: 'Take heart; get up, he is calling *you*.' To 'take heart' is clearly more substantial than the NIV's translation of the text as 'Cheer up!')

So, when Isaiah represents God's instruction to 'Comfort, O comfort my people', he is indulging in more than spiritual sentiment. He is drawing on a tradition that permeates the character of the whole biblical narrative. Go back to Job, devastated by a series of personal and family disasters – illness, bereavement and loss. Three friends took it on themselves to 'console and comfort' him (Job 2.11), but they did this by sitting in silence with him for seven days and seven nights. Comfort came from their silent presence, not platitudes.

Look ahead to the New Testament and we find the apostle Paul constantly comforting young Christians, but not by urging convenience or self-preserving escapism. Instead, he does this by emphasizing endurance and perseverance under suffering. 'To comfort', then, is not to create an illusion, to urge some escape or offer wishful sentiment; rather, it is to face reality, encourage determination and endure.

So, to return to Isaiah 40, the exiles have endured decades of exile. Their children have been born in exile and know no other reality. There looks to be no possibility in the short term of a return to the homeland – and why would they want to be uprooted again anyway and return to what is no longer home, except in notional terms? Isaiah begs the question: what would have been heard as words of comfort by the exiles? He is consistent with the biblical thread we have glanced at above. The words that follow – fleshing out the notion of comfort intended here – do not promise instant satisfaction or some *deus ex machina* that would resolve all problems and make everything safe again. There is no nostalgia here – the sort of fantasy thinking that leads to slogans such as 'Make America Great Again' or 'Take back control' (when it was never lost in the first place). Comfort happens in the real world of time and place.

The content of the comfort is to be seen in the words that follow the injunction: 'Speak tenderly to Jerusalem, and cry to her that she has served her term, that her penalty is paid, that she has received from the LORD's hand double for all her sins' (40.2). Isaiah reinforces reality: the time is coming, but not yet, when you shall be liberated, but remember why you are here in the first place. Yes, you have suffered, but you are now going to be asked to imagine, articulate and work towards a future that looks ridiculous. Are you up for it?

This is important. It assumes that the exiles will take responsibility for what is to come – that liberation and return will demand of them a commitment to action, shaping the future, ordering their common life in such a way as not to repeat the sins of the past. For them to be comforted is to have demands made of them – demands for honest reflection, responsibility for past choices and the acceptance of obligation for the future.

Comforting Lord, strengthen us to hear your call, to acknowledge our past and commit to shaping a future of justice and mercy. Amen.

WEEK 1: FRIDAY

Hearing and speaking (40.21)

Have you not known? Have you not heard?

The world of the twenty-first century might well be described as a cacophony of media and voices aggressively competing for the attention of our eyes and ears, our imaginations and commitment, our intellects and our will. I grew up with two and then three television stations and these only broadcast for a limited number of hours every day. My grandchildren are growing up in a digital world of constant and inescapable noise and images; a world we are creating seemingly without the moral competence to understand and control it. Life is complex, temptations are everywhere, distractions threaten to keep us anaesthetized from what really matters in life.

Yet the question of which voices we should listen to is not a new one. The technology might be different, the quantity infinitely greater and the volume louder than nearly three thousand years ago, but the question was there even then.

In Isaiah's (more limited and circumscribed) world, the people were offered a range of choices for their communal, national and individual life. What we read in the first 39 chapters of Isaiah is an account of how people, offered different and competing visions of how they might shape their future, find it hard to listen to what they

21

basically don't want to hear. I suspect human nature then was not dissimilar to human nature today.

And if those who refused to hear the warnings of chapters 1—39 were anything to go by, why should the exiles of 40—55 be any different? If inconvenient words of warning were difficult to hear at home, then why should words of comfort be any easier for exiles to heed in the face of 'reality'?

This is a situation that is not uncommon for any other people in any other generation. The exiles found it difficult (maybe even rather absurd) to hear words of comfort and encouragement when the evidence all around them told a different story, but it is the same for us today. For instance (and to take a contemporary and contentious example), how are we to discern the word of the Lord in our own context: Brexit, the rise of the Far Right in Europe, the Trump–Putin nexus, the rise of China as an economic and military power? Are we to discern the word of the Lord as the warnings of Isaiah 1—39 or the comfort and encouragement of 40—55? How are we to know who is telling the truth about what and who is lying or misrepresenting reality? Whom should we trust when the voices compete for our attention and our commitment?

For me, this was a very real question at the time of and following the referendum on the European Union in 2016 in the United Kingdom. Immediately after the declaration that the UK had voted to leave the EU, I tweeted, 'The people have spoken. But, we don't know what they have said.' As we are only too well aware, the debates, claims, counter-claims, criticisms and accusations flowed in volume in the ensuing couple of years, creating for many an utter confusion of voices claiming that theirs is the only truth. By mostly supporting Remain, bishops were accused of being out of touch with the dispossessed in their dioceses and failing to understand the real grievances of ordinary people. However, this was to confuse understanding with agreement. It simply does not follow that understanding people's grievances must lead to agreeing with their views. The prophetic task is – and always has been – to speak the truth as one understands it, prayerfully and intelligently, whatever people think about it.

Should German Christians in the 1930s have simply said, 'Well, people are very upset about economics and are hugely keen on Adolf Hitler. Therefore, we must go along with the view of the people and support the National Socialists'? Of course not. The hard job is to discern what the will of the Lord is and not confuse it with the will of the people. If the will of the Lord crosses that of the people, then so be it: those who speak it will suffer the consequences – just as the prophets of the Old Testament always did in their day.

Now, this is where we need to distinguish between our speaking and our listening. Those called to speak must do so with moral, spiritual and intellectual integrity, following prayerful listening, especially to the voices that might be unsympathetic to one's own instincts. However, all of us are called to listen – in particular to the voices that we find difficult – but then make a judgement in humility.

Of course, this is easier said than done. We are bombarded today with appeals through music, television, radio, websites, social media and so on. There is no peace, and the place of sober reflection is in danger of being displaced by the demand for instant judgement (often with the consequence of instant abuse rather than intelligent and respectful engagement). If we didn't recognize it before, we certainly should now: information is not the same as knowledge and knowledge is not the same as wisdom.

If listening to unpopular or unwelcome news was difficult for the exiles in the eighth century BC, it is no easier for us today, in a very different age and culture. The (eventual) exiles could only have heard the bad news of Isaiah 1—39 if they had first questioned the voices telling them all would be well. The warnings had to be listened to and not simply rejected because they were inconvenient to well-established prejudices that hid reality. Likewise, here in chapter 40, for words of comfort to be heard by the exiles would demand a daring openness to the possibility of hope and redemption – despite the evidence of the world and their experience now.

This becomes the challenge for God's people of any time and place: are we really open to the 'word of the Lord' or only when it coincides with what we want to hear? An archbishop once said to me: 'When they ask me to lead, they really mean that I must go where they want to see me go. If I do not, then I am not a leader. When they ask me to speak prophetically, they mean they want to hear me say loudly what they want to hear me say. If I say something else, I am not being prophetic.'

The same challenge lies here in Advent. As we await the Messiah's coming, do we try to fit him into a rigid shape that is formed by our prejudices or preferences or are we open to being surprised, challenged, shaken up – to 'repent'?

Lord of all hopefulness, help us to open our ears to discern your word (of warning or hope) amid the cacophony of voices that we hear. Amen.

WEEK 1: SATURDAY

Learning to wait (40.31)

Those who wait for the LORD shall renew their strength.

I understand why some organizers of carol services leave off the final verse of 'Once in Royal David's City': 'Where like stars His children crowned all in white shall wait around.' It picks up on the contrast between Jesus' birth in a stable and his reign in heaven, but the 'waiting around' just sounds a bit aimless.

However, waiting is active and not merely passive. To wait is not to do nothing. When Isaiah states that 'those who wait for the LORD shall renew their strength', he does not mean us to imagine just hanging around, hoping that the Lord might do something interesting.

When I was a child, I had to learn to wait for the seasons to rotate. Unless they were in season, you couldn't buy strawberries, for example. So we had to wait for the rhythm of the year to run its course before we could again taste this sweet fruit. The waiting (for most of the year) made the arrival of strawberries in the shops all the more wonderful. The anticipation grew as time went by. Today, we can buy strawberries on any day of the year.

The loss of the rhythms of the year is a casualty of modern commerce and impatient people. Instant access to information via the internet, social media and mobile technology means that everything has speeded up. This has brought untold benefits but, like all good things in life, it has also come at a cost. The world never sleeps. Our eyes and ears are bombarded by images and demands for our attention. We bury ourselves in the interconnectedness of relationships and communication, which threatens to strike us at any moment of the day or night. Maybe, without realizing it was happening to us, we have forgotten how to wait.

It should not come as a surprise, then, that this frantic and complex world is seeing an upsurge in the numbers of people wanting to book into retreats – longing for the right sort of solitude, fellowship, silence or space. As Advent invites us to slow down, relisten to the story of God and the world, make space for the preparation of heart and mind before the quiet irruption of God into the material world in Jesus, we might well hear that beautiful phrase by the Welsh poet R. S. Thomas: 'the meaning is in the waiting'. (Paula Gooder's wonderful book, with these words used as its title, helps us to explore what this substantial waiting might involve.)

Yet the preposition that follows the verb is also significant. I grew up with the King James Bible and the reference to 'they that wait upon the LORD'. This always sounded to me like something that happens in a restaurant. Modern versions read 'wait for the LORD' and this seems more accurate as well as more suggestive. What does 'waiting for the Lord' imply?

One implication is simply that God will not be rushed. We have to learn to wait for God's time – the Kairos – and we cannot rush, engineer or force it. It suggests that God is ahead of us, calling us to take time to follow him, but also that he is behind us, moving more slowly than we might like. The point is, though, it is our job to wait for God and not God's job to jump to our demands. As Socrates reportedly put it, 'the best sauce for food is hunger'.

Kosuke Koyama was the first Asian theologian I ever came across when studying theology. After a particularly difficult pastoral episode during my curacy in Kendal, I had 24 hours in silence at a convent in the south of England. Browsing in the library, I came across his book of meditations entitled *Three Mile an Hour God*. In it, Koyama describes the people of Israel being led into the desert after the Exodus. He muses that the first thing to happen when we enter a desert is that we slow down. He goes on to suggest that it is only once we have slowed down to walking pace – 3 m.p.h. – that we discover this is the pace God is moving at.

I took this thought a bit further in a book I wrote about hope. The first thing most of us want to do if we enter a desert (actual or metaphorical – it could be spiritual depression or the feeling that God is absent, for example) is to get out of it as quickly as possible. However, Koyama is clear that we must not try to escape, to run away from the dry place, but stick with it and stay so long that the slowing down teaches us to wait and look differently for where God is and what he might be saying or doing.

This is what waiting for God is about.

If we read the Bible in order to get the big picture, the grand sweep of its narrative, we discover that time takes time. Humanity arrived millions of years after the Big Bang. God calls a people to live in the world in such a way as to reflect (or even embody) his character and concerns. When they go into exile in Egypt, they are there for over 400 years. Imagine that. Generations of people have known no other life than that of being immigrants in Egypt. When they are liberated in the Exodus, they then spend 40 years in a desert wandering round in circles . . . until they learn that we cannot live by bread alone but need the word and presence of God. During those years, a generation of the liberated died out, taking with them their short-term and shortsighted nostalgia and fantasies. Throughout the exiles of the eighth and sixth centuries before Christ, God apparently did not rush to end his people's suffering and anxieties – even their religious anxieties; history took time and God's promised judgement was worked out not by magic but by history taking its course. We have to learn to live with the consequences of our idolatries and God will not be rushed.

That is why here in Isaiah 40 the exiles are encouraged to wait for God but not give up hope. Their strength will be renewed because they are drawn by faith in the God of their history, who has proved himself to be faithful in the past. Not rushed, but faithful.

There are no shortcuts to waiting. The waiting for God is a renewing experience because in it we let go of the frantic demand for significance and learn to inhabit the space into which God will eventually come. As someone once put it, when you are in the desert, look for the flowers that grow only in the desert; if you only look for daffodils, you will be constantly frustrated and will miss out on the uniqueness of what only the desert place can offer.

Lord God, when we feel bereft or that you are absent from us, teach us the patience to wait for you . . . and to spot the signs of your coming among us again. Amen.

Week 2: Easy idols

WEEK 2: SUNDAY

Introduction to the week

Jesus encouraged his friends to fulfil what had always been the vocation of God's people: to love the Lord your God with all your heart and mind and strength – and your neighbour as yourself (Luke 10.27, quoting Deuteronomy 6.5). This was never about individual personal piety (although it includes this), but about a community of people who tried to look at God, the world and us through the eyes of the God who had created and rescued them. In other words, it recognized that we need each other to keep on keeping on in the discipleship business.

The problem we have is that there are a million distractions from loving God and our neighbour in his name. The story of biblical Israel is one of diverted attention. We forget quickly God's faithfulness over time and want only quick satisfaction of our shorter-term needs or desires. As the writer of Ecclesiastes recognizes, there is nothing new under the sun. It is not hard to spot the places and times when we have been unfaithful to God's call and too easily distracted by the attractions of small gods – idols.

This week we shall explore a little of what this looks like, why we do it and what we might do about it – together.

WEEK 2: MONDAY

Small gods (41.29)

Their images are empty wind.

The late-lamented Terry Pratchett, creator and sustainer of the fictional Discworld, punctured many popular perceptions of God and religion in his very funny and astute book, *Small Gods*. A brilliant satire, a central element in the story is this: the more people believe in the gods, the bigger they grow; the less they are believed in, the more they shrink. So, the gods need people's belief more than the people need to believe (and, in fact, they only believe in order to avoid trouble or for a peaceful life). The whole story is funny, but sad: sad, particularly, that religion is open to such a sharp and too-often justified critique.

However, the title itself suggests broader thinking. The unique thing about Judaism as described in the Old Testament is its monotheistic claims. In contrast to other religions, Yahweh was no mere tribal deity, looking after the interests or threatening the well-being of particular groups of people. Rather, he was the Creator, Sustainer and Lover of the entire cosmos. A bold claim and one that was bound to cause endless conflicts. Now it haunts the exiles who, sitting by the banks of Babylonian rivers, are taunted by their oppressors to sing songs of their great God who has allowed them to languish in captivity: some great God this is (Psalm 137).

Isaiah does not spare any blushes. In his books he keeps coming back to the fundamental problem of God's people: they forget their vocation and lose sight of the God who calls them by name; their eyes are turned too easily by lesser attractions. In drawing attention to this propensity, Isaiah has a lot of material to draw on. Go back to the Garden of Eden again: there human beings, mortal and creaturely, can't resist the temptation to want more – to be like God . . . now.

Leap ahead to the national trauma of racial and ethnic oppression in Egypt – a place of refuge from famine that eventually becomes a place of captivity for over 400 years – and the liberation we call the Exodus. A people who couldn't save themselves find a way to freedom under the reluctant leadership of Moses (a murderer)

and are led, miraculously, out of Egypt towards a land of promise. They are only out of captivity for five minutes before they start
complaining that desert food (which keeps them alive, if not fat) is
rubbish and maybe things weren't so bad in Egypt after all. At one
point, the ever-patient Moses leaves them in the desert in order to
go up a mountain – from which he will soon descend with the Ten
Commandments – and comes back to find that they have melted
their gold and designed a golden calf (the animal, not the lower part
of a leg) on which to lay their hopes and prayers.

No wonder, then, that Isaiah has warned the people in the first
part of his prophecy that this constant loss of vocation will end in
tears. Read chapter 1 and it is all laid bare: you do evil and are cor-
rupt; your solemn religious assemblies have become a sad joke;
you have forgotten that your God cares little about sacrifices and
observance of religious ritual when he then sees you selling justice,
oppressing the poor and despising the vulnerable in your community. He doesn't let up. 'Their land is filled with idols; they bow down
to the work of their hands, to what their own fingers have made'
(2.8). And it is both the stupidity and the arrogance of it that offends
Isaiah as he exposes the ridiculousness of such a cheap exchange: the
Creator for the creation.

That is what Isaiah reminds them when, in promising in his second book (40—55) that release from exile is surely coming, he mocks
their tendency willingly to make objects in which they invest god-
like virtues: 'No, they are all a delusion; their works are nothing;
their images are empty wind' (41.29).

If the people of Isaiah's time found it so easy to be distracted by
small gods, shouldn't we have learned by now not to fall into the
same convenient trap? Yet we do. Maybe we don't make idols of
stone, wood or metal in the same way, but we have some very contemporary distractions and seductions that turn us away from the
call of God the Creator, Sustainer and Lover of all, and invest our
attention and affections in cheaper options.

It would be easy at this point to construct a list of such contemporary idols. They might include the usual suspects of money, power and sex. However, we need to look harder to identify the idols of which we are sometimes unaware or those that have emerged from objects of love and began as just and right and noble, but have been gradually corrupted. We should not point a finger at the exiles until we have done this imaginative exercise for ourselves, perhaps thinking about which idols we now worship: affluence, security, national identity or self-preservation (of self, community or race, for example).

This is not an easy exercise but, having attempted it honestly, we will be in a better place to understand and think about the very contemporary human experience addressed by Isaiah 2,500 years ago in a different context and culture.

Lord God, give us the courage to look deeply into our own affections and discern where we have swapped worship of the Creator for a smaller god. Amen.

WEEK 2: TUESDAY

My God? (41.9)

I have chosen you.

The social media generation has invented a new language of abbreviations and icons (emojis). One that always makes me cringe is 'OMG', meaning 'Oh my God!' It has become almost a default exclamation for any experience deemed worthy of remark. Why? OK, it is concise and seems to be used in its longer form by almost everyone everywhere; but why this particular expression? A brief exploration might link us back to the matter of cheap idols and contemporary culture that we looked at yesterday.

First, we need to note that there is a fundamental dynamic to the relationship between God and his people. God does the choosing: 'I have chosen you . . . do not fear, for I am with you, do not be afraid, for I am your God' (41.9–10). Whereas people choose their cheap idols, God makes it clear that he is the one who does the choosing. This matters enormously. If God chooses his people – those whom he calls to bear his name, reflect his character and priorities and give up their lives that the world might see and touch and encounter this God – then their identity is tied up with how they respond in love to his calling. They did not choose God from among other options; he chose them. That changes everything.

Look ahead in the Bible and you will hear Jesus making the same claim to his disciples. In the address to his friends prior to his betrayal and crucifixion, Jesus says explicitly, 'You did not choose me but I chose you' (John 15.16). The implications of that action are many. For example, if Jesus does the choosing of his friends, inviting them to walk with him into uncertainty, then their job is to walk together and not apart from one another. In the Gospels, Jesus does the calling and his friends do the following . . . together. They do not get to veto who else is chosen by Jesus. They do not get to impose conditions on who is called by Jesus to go with them: their witness is surely to be found in the way, despite their differences and divergences, they walk together with Jesus. Now, doesn't that change the way we think about the Church and who belongs to it?

So, Jesus is here reflecting the primary relationship of God with his people: he chooses them and their part in it is to respond. All they can do is respond, not initiate. In this sense, it could be said that, for us today, being a Christian is simply a lived response to having been called by Jesus, rooted in gratitude and faith. We are 'chosen' not only to live God's way – justly, humbly, sacrificially, faithfully – but also to resist the temptation or tendency to follow other paths that are more convenient or comfortable for us.

Where, then, does idolatry connect with the fact of having been chosen by God? We might well capture Isaiah's concerns if we go back to the common exclamation, 'Oh my God!'

To speak of 'my God' assumes that God is either a personal commodity or possession or I have chosen my own god. In a Western culture that is increasingly narcissistic and self-referential, this should perhaps come as no surprise, but the constant use of the phrase might reveal more to us than we might at first think. Do I create or shape God in my own image? Do I owe allegiance to God only so long as he does what is convenient to me or offers a quicker and better service than anyone else? Do I unwittingly assume that God's priorities coincide with or reinforce my own prejudices and ways of thinking about the world and other people? For example, would Jesus vote Labour, Conservative, Liberal Democrat . . . or none of the above?

All this should lead us to subject our views of God, the world, politics, economics, values and so on to the scrutiny of the biblical witness. How is it possible to pervert justice (or allow the perversion of justice to be institutionalized in our own society) and at the same time sing songs of God's priorities for the poor and marginalized and oppressed? How do we blank out the words of the prophets or of Jesus when we find it more appropriate to prioritize other values or behaviours? Try asking this God to 'forgive us our sins' without the 'as we forgive those who sin against us'; or consider the rightness of giving access to justice to those with money to buy it, while cutting out those who do not have the means . . . and then read Amos or Isaiah.

This is the problem we all have: we reduce the God of the cosmos to 'my god' or the god of my convenience. Yet that is not just to be seen in our wider culture, where the language of idolatry might not be popular, but the reality is evident. It is there to be seen and heard in the worship of the Church. Whereas Jesus addresses himself mostly to his followers (plural), we hear and receive his words as given to 'me', as an individual in my own walk with him. Isaiah, while inevitably calling to account individuals as children of Yahweh, addresses himself to the people collectively. It is how they shape their common life and worship together that is at the heart of his concern.

Should it be of some concern to us, then, that so many contemporary worship songs have us addressing God in terms of 'I', 'me' and 'my'? Should we not be using the language of 'we', which, in continual use, then shapes our unconscious assumptions about God and us (not just God and me) and frequently provokes a certain discomfort with the contradictions between God's way and ours? Or, to come at it from a different angle, how do I prioritize my part for the greater good of the whole over the blessing I personally seek?

God who calls his people to love and serve him by loving and serving other people, so shape our hearts and minds that we might reflect the nature of the God who calls us. Amen.

WEEK 2: WEDNESDAY

Any dream will do? (41.29)

They are all a delusion.

I think Andrew Lloyd Webber is brilliant. I once met him to discuss his plans to launch a television search for someone to play Jesus in a revival of *Jesus Christ Superstar*. Understandably, he had concerns about how Christians might respond to reality television approaching Jesus in this way. I thought it was a gift for the Church. Searching for Jesus in prime time, but begging the question throughout: what sort of Jesus are you looking for? How could any Christian with an ounce of evangelistic imagination object to that?

However, this has to be set against the damage done by Joseph. Not Mary's husband but the young man who was given an amazing technicolour dreamcoat by his father. Lloyd Webber wrote the music

34

and Tim Rice the lyrics of the drama enacted in a million schools and local amateur theatres around the country. Hugely popular (and deservedly so, in my humble opinion), it put to a wonderful tune an idea that is so ludicrous it is a wonder it ever got through: 'any dream will do'. Too harsh? Isn't the emphasis rightly on the need for everyone to have a dream at some point in their life?

Just think about it for a minute. We'll start with the positive. Human beings are born to imagine and to wonder. It is this constant nagging sense that we matter fundamentally which awakens our imaginations and our minds to the possibility of there being more to life than mere stuff and things. Curiosity insists that we must explore and question and experience and push at boundaries. We are born to dream, to be drawn by a vision of a better world and a better life. That is all good. But will *any* dream really do?

Our contemporary culture, shaped more recently by what is often called 'identity politics', puts the individual at the centre of everything and insists that the world must be shaped around one's needs and preferences. That this leads to unworkable chaos should be obvious. It is this way of seeing the world which leads quickly to the assertion that, as long as you are sincere, that is good enough. Any dream will do . . . as long as you have a dream. However, what if your dream is of racial domination, national imperialism or ethnic cleansing? Is this so if it is of something less violent, such as everyone having access to material satisfaction (even if this anaesthetizes the harder and deeper questions of human meaning and collective responsibility) or that my life should be comfortable, despite this coming at the expense of everybody else's life?

You get the point. However good the musical, it has sown in the minds of a generation a fundamental untruth of human living, for any dream will *not* do. Being sincere about something is not enough, especially if the object of our sincere belief is a fantasy. In other words, we need to be somewhat more critical of the voices we hear and the things we assume about what to believe and how to live in the light of them.

How does this apply to Isaiah? Well, the people addressed by the first 39 chapters of the prophecy were consistently and continually warned about being distracted by cheaper gods – idols that could never deliver what they promised. Clearly, there were plenty of other 'prophets' who made a living out of telling people what they wanted to hear, rather than insisting on what they perceived to be true. It is always easier to keep everyone happy – easier to collude with a collective fantasy than to be the one bringing unwelcome or unpopular news. Isaiah and the other prophets of the Old Testament knew all about this. They had no illusions about 'itching ears' and the cost of not scratching them.

Take, for example, a contentious political debate in the country: should the Church of England come down on one side or the other? Should bishops try to discern the will of God for one side or the other when Christians are as divided as the country? In my experience, we get written off as traitors. However, not to agree should not be characterized as not to understand or not to listen. It is remarkable how many people align God's will, the truth and the Church's leadership responsibility with the line *I* find most conducive.

Part of the role of God's people is to recognize 'empty wind' and 'delusions' when they come across them but, as we all know, it is harder in practice than when reading Isaiah. Other people's delusions are always easier to identify and mock than are our own. If anything, a reading of Isaiah should invite us to be a little humbler, a little more open to seeing differently (even to our own inconvenience or discomfort), a little more understanding of those who strive to discern the will of God but come to a different conclusion, and a little more committed to testing the dreams we have on the bench of God's character and priorities as we read them in Scripture.

God of truth, grant us the wisdom to see you more clearly, to stay faithful to you and not be distracted by delusions, and to be courageous in telling the truth ... whatever the cost. Amen.

WEEK 2: THURSDAY

Seeing and hearing? (42.20)

His ears are open, but he does not hear.

I remember the day we realized our eldest son was seriously colour blind. We were at my in-laws, looking out of their huge living-room window down the long autumnal garden at the bright red berries sparkling among all the greenery. It was beautiful. My son was looking at the same view, but couldn't see any berries at all. (Try playing snooker with him . . .)

I also remember when I was a child, hearing about the family down the road who were visited several times every week by two elderly spinster aunts. The wife found herself in a surprising conversation with her (southern) neighbour about how to get rid of the ants. It was only after discussing the relative effectiveness of using ant powder or pouring boiling water over them that they realized they were talking at cross purposes – pronunciation didn't distinguish between 'aunt' and 'ant'. (I don't endorse either method, just in case you get distracted by cruelty to insects.)

We have all been there, haven't we? We think we are listening and seeing but, if all goes well, discover later that we misheard or failed to see the real thing. This, in part, is what Isaiah is exposing: his people too easily hear what they want to hear and see what they want to see. This means, of course, that they then filter out of their seeing and hearing those things they don't like or want. Do they do this deliberately? I would suggest that people don't always do this consciously but need to have it pointed out from the outside that this is, in fact, what is actually happening . . . whether they realize it or not.

There are two elements behind this phenomenon here in Isaiah 42: (a) the people's self-pity and (b) God's shock-treatment.

The first is that the people have probably been complaining that God has forgotten them and no longer sees them or hears their cries. They are in exile and God seems not to recognize their plight, their misery or their lack of a future. Reminded every day (by the local Babylonians) of the apparent misguidedness of their faith in Yahweh, they complain that Yahweh pays no attention to their suffering. Perhaps they can't hear the words of comfort in 42.6–9, including the restatement of vocation:

> I have called you . . . I have taken you . . . and kept you; I have given you as a covenant to the people, a light to the nations, to open the eyes that are blind, to bring out the prisoners from the dungeon, from the prison those who sit in darkness.

Wallowing in their own self-pity, they are unable to hear Yahweh when he is more than paying attention to them. So the charge is pressed: your ears are closed to the whispered language of newness and freedom; your eyes look, but do not see what is before them – the God who is present, but not in the way you thought he should be.

This raises all sorts of questions about the human propensity to miss the point. Leap ahead into the Gospels and we hear Jesus addressing the very people who studied the Scriptures and were most diligent about understanding theology: 'You search the scriptures because you think that in them you have eternal life; and it is they that testify on my behalf. Yet you refuse to come to me to have life' (John 5.39–40). In other words, what you are looking for so earnestly (and religiously/devotedly) is standing right in front of you and you can't see him. As a Christian leader whose job involves searching and teaching the Scriptures, this verse haunts me every day; being close to the text doesn't mean being open to what it says.

The second element is harder. Having issued repeated words of comfort to these miserable exiles (who cannot or dare not hear and see?), Isaiah goes back again and again to hammering home their fundamental problem: you who are called to release others from their prisons are, in fact, locked up in your own! The door is open but you are so caught up in your own self-pitying complaining that you can't walk through it. So how are you ever to fulfil your true vocation (which will open you to God's newness) if you prefer to stay with the familiar convenience of your own gloom and negativity?

I think this is familiar stuff. In one sense, we might describe our self-pity as an idol – something that distracts us from hearing the inviting call of God and seeing what the world might look like if we took this invitation seriously.

The final observation here must surely be that we need each other in order to check whether or not what we see and hear is accurate. (Yes, the problem for the exiles was that they collectively reinforced their common misery – the downside of having each other to listen to.) So when the lone voice comes out of the desert and whispers hope into despair, I might not hear it because my ears are closed . . . but someone else might do. Am I open to hearing surprising news of criticism or comfort, sometimes from unusual sources, and opening my eyes and ears to new possibilities?

Lord, give your people the imagination and courage to open their ears and eyes to your word and your face, that we might be a people of defiant hope, not colluders in our own limitations. Amen.

WEEK 2: FRIDAY

One God (44.6)

Besides me there is no god.

We now have to dig deep into our imaginations again. Remember the exiles, sitting on the banks of their oppressors' rivers and being mocked for their absurd faith in a God who has clearly deserted them? Remember how hard it must have been to maintain belief and trust in a God who is silent, who has let you be defeated and apparently now refuses to come to your aid? You might manage it for a few days; but how do you hang on to this after decades of ridicule from your mockers and no evidence that your God is even there, let alone cares?

This is where the outrageous claim about Yahweh comes into sharp relief against the cultural and religious situation of Isaiah's time. Ancient societies were largely polytheistic – that is, they entertained a plurality of gods, tribal deities whose purpose was to guide and defend the people who worshipped them. If you were to look through Babylonian eyes, for example, you would unconsciously look for evidence that your gods were on your side and doing their job on your behalf. You keep the gods happy and they will keep their side of the bargain. So, if you are dominant and your society seems to be on top, it is reasonable to conclude that your god is bigger than other people's gods.

How, then, are the Babylonians to cope with a people who sit in exiled captivity, yet keep singing the songs of their God who claims to be the only God and the Creator/Sustainer of the cosmos? You can see why they had a bit of a laugh.

However, it is this bold claim, uttered in defiance of 'reality', that defines the people of Yahweh and challenges the powers that be. It touches on the repeated experience of those who deem the claim to be credible in the face of silence.

First, Israel's God is no tribal deity. This is a God who breaks all the rules and claims to be for everyone. This God does not compete with idols but, rather, asks people to demand more from their idols, knowing that inanimate bits of wood and metal cannot deliver. God's people are to have a big view of the God of the cosmos – a view that sees through immediate circumstances and dares to trust anyway. They are to refuse obeisance to made-up gods and idols made of stuff and hold on to the God whose story defines them as a people with a unique identity. To be blunt, they are God's people because they are human beings made in God's image; this precedes any national, ethnic or religious identity markers.

Second, this God will not be rushed into proving himself in order to keep people happy. God's people therefore have to maintain a defiance that will always look silly to the watching world but will prove to be right in the end. Even in exile, God is God and has not abandoned them. Even in captivity, God promises liberation as history takes its course. Even when the evidence of their eyes speaks of absence and silence, God beckons them to stand up to quick-fix solutions to human questions of meaning and purpose and allow themselves to be held on to by the God who takes a longer view.

Of course, the claim of exclusivity was no more popular then than it is today. In a contemporary world of 'any dream will do' pluralism, exclusive claims are met with mockery and accusations of arrogance. But Christians today have to grow the confidence of Isaiah's exiles in politely declining to bow to lesser gods, humbly accepting the mockery and giving allegiance only to the Creator and Sustainer of the cosmos. Our vocation is, however, not arrogantly to claim exclusivity of favour from God, but to live up to the outwardly ridiculous call to lay down our lives in order that the world might see just who this God is and what this God is about.

So exclusive claims by God or about God should bring us back to that central vocation and responsibility: to love as God loves and to open the eyes of the blind to the glory hidden from those who only look down at their feet, locked in some need for satisfaction now, fearful of a future that seems to threaten. God's people should be free to live now in the light of a tomorrow that defies the evidence and beckons us to take God and his promises seriously. Exile now does not mean exile for ever.

Lord of all, grasp our hearts and minds with a vision of your eternal glory so that we can live now in hope of a future that is yours. Amen.

WEEK 2: SATURDAY

Shaping a future (45.9)

What are you making?

I used to represent the Archbishop of Canterbury at one or two global interfaith conferences. In this role I went a number of times to Kazakhstan, a country that seems alien and remote to many in Europe. Yet this young country has seen remarkable growth in the last two decades. After it had broken free from Soviet domination in 1991, the self-declared President Nursultan Nazarbayev got a grip on the country and forged its future, opening it up to foreign investment and interest. He also built a new capital city in Astana – a very long way from the traditional capital, Almaty, which lies too close to the Chinese border.

Flying back from Astana one time, I was musing why all the young people I met in Kazakhstan were so strongly supportive of their President and so fiercely proud of their young nation. I would remind them of corruption and power-grabbing – it is easier to build a city if no one has the power to object, for example – and they would brush these aside because they could see that life was improving so rapidly for all the people. For these young people, the world was opening up, the future offering opportunities they had never expected, the present bringing employment, material growth and hope for a bright future unimagined by their parents and grandparents.

I would then land back in Frankfurt or London and ask what the young people of Europe were building. I found it hard to find an answer. Kazakh young people were building a new country, full of opportunity, a future they were energized to create and shape. It seemed to me at the time that, in Europe, our young people were simply being expected to hold on to a legacy of a post-war European settlement and weren't actually building anything. The contrast might have been unfair, but I record it because it is what bothered me then (and still does).

This comes to mind because, as the proverb puts it: 'Where there is no vision, the people perish' (29.18, KJV). If people do not commit themselves to building a future, they do not remain neutral but slowly atrophy and die. Part of the mandate given to human beings in the creation narratives of Genesis 1—11 is to cultivate the earth – that is, to grow things, to develop culture, to explore the created order and reflect the God who brings order out of chaos.

So the question mockingly articulated in Isaiah 45.9 ('Does the clay say to the one who fashions it, "What are you making"?'), in a chapter that will shock the exiles, is capable of many readings. According to this chapter, God is going to use a pagan ruler to be the agent of his liberation, thus compelling the exiles once again to acknowledge the sovereign and unimprisoned will of the Creator God to shape the world. Why, asks Isaiah, do you think it is clever to argue with the Creator? What sort of relationship is this that sees the clay questioning the potter about his intentions?

Well, it isn't quite as simple as that. The biblical story encourages us to argue and wrestle with God – never simply to remain indifferent or apathetic. But this question, aimed at human beings, is a fundamental one: what are you making? For what sort of future do you take responsibility? Are you merely ambling through life, hoping not to get too bruised by the arrows of fortune, or are you shaping a future to look something like one that is faithful to God's character?

Sometimes, especially when the going gets tough or people are disappointed, I wonder if human beings fall into one of two categories: whingers and shapers. There are those who complain about the lot they have been handed in life – always a victim of other people's wills and therefore never responsible. And there are those who, conscious of their own failings and limitations, still get on and try to shape the world (or the Church), thus taking responsibility for what then befalls them. I think we all face a choice, every day, of which category we wish to fall into. The former is debilitating and corrosive of society; the latter is constructive and energizing all round.

This challenge is going to become very real for the exiles. When they return to their homeland, what sort of a society will they then establish? How will they engage with those whose land it now is – the generations who have inhabited the space since the exiles disappeared from view? Will their religious practice change because their circumstances are now new or will they try to return to how it was before they were deported? Has their view of God changed in the light of experience or have they pickled God in the aspic of religious memory?

Anyone who bears God's name has to ask the question: what am I making and am I willing to take responsibility for it, come what may?

Lord, you call each of us to be shapers of your kingdom where we live – active agents of grace and articulators of hope. Help us to be faithful and responsible in fulfilling this vocation. Amen.

Week 3: Fear and faith

WEEK 3: SUNDAY

Introduction to the week

In the last two weeks we have begun to explore a little of the context of the exiles to whom Isaiah addresses his prophecy. We have also dug imaginatively into some of the questions raised by their experience and the challenge they pose to faith in a God who claims to be for us. In one sense, we have to live with this before we can begin to understand what is going on for Isaiah or for us.

In Advent, we anticipate the coming of the Messiah among us. We have to do that hard trick of living with the story as it unravels, trying not to run ahead to what could not have been known by the characters we encounter in the story . . . yet, at the same time, read back into the present from what we know is coming at the end (which turns out to be a new beginning and not an end at all). So it is with Isaiah's exiles. If we are to understand the mental wallpaper of those longing for the coming of the messiah – and their disappointment when he doesn't turn out to look like the messiah they had expected – we must live with their experience and try to relate it to ours in a very different time and place.

This week we will look at the sense of perspective crucial to the hearing of good news by those used only to bad news.

WEEK 3: MONDAY

Real fear (41.10, 13, 14)

Do not fear . . .

I was doing *Pause for Thought* on the Chris Evans Show on BBC Radio 2 one morning when the musical guest in the studio was Billy Ocean. I hadn't heard of him for years. He was great, but I took the opportunity in my script to paraphrase one of his most famous songs, 'When the going gets tough, the tough get going.' I changed it to, 'When the going gets tough, the tough write poetry.' He laughed.

I was referring, of course, to the prophets and psalmists of the Hebrew Scriptures who in their poetry went to the heart of human emotions and experience. There are still people around who will tell you that the Psalms are songs of praise, and some of them are. Around two-thirds of them, however, are songs of torment, lament, complaint, fear and hope. I doubt if the writer being hunted for his life would have set the words of Psalm 42 to a jaunty little tune.

What comes out of the prophets and Psalms is an expression of the raw fear that hopes, but wobbles – that isn't sure of some guaranteed deliverance from trouble. Some songs end in a defiant statement of promise but others do not resolve at all. This, I think, accords with most people's experience of life at some point – just hanging in there.

When thinking about Isaiah's words of promise and hope, we need to stop again and read between the lines. Three times in chapter 41 the exiles are told not to fear. Though God seems absent and suspicion of your oppressors is entirely justified, do not let fear get a hold on you: 'do not fear, for I am with you, do not be afraid, for I am your God' (41.10). But, given that there are reasonable grounds for fear, isn't this just manipulative fantasy?

Try chapter 43 and the oft-quoted verses of deliverance:

Do not fear, for I have redeemed you; I have called you by
name, you are mine. When you pass through the waters, I will
be with you; and through the rivers, they shall not overwhelm
you; when you walk through fire you shall not be burned, and
the flame shall not consume you.
(43.1–2)

That's the good news. The bad news (when we read between the lines)
is this: you are going to face waters, rivers and fire. In other words,
you cannot know what it is to be unafraid from a distance; you will
have to experience it as you go through the torment.

Well, shouldn't God be sparing them any further torment?
Haven't they suffered enough in exile? Haven't they already lost too
much without having now to face further pain?

The thing about the Bible is that it tells the truth and never seeks to
seduce anyone into being faithful to God. Here we get utter realism.
In real life in the real world, even deliverance from one form of suffering does not mean that you will never suffer again. Life carries on.
You are mortal and live in a contingent world in which cells replicate,
some mutate, cancers grow, people do terrible things, circumstances
can't be controlled, life can be rubbish – and there are no exceptions.

That, in fact, goes to the heart of biblical faith: it does not depend
on good outcomes but commits anyway. Richard Rohr put it like this:
'Faith isn't for overcoming obstacles; it's for experiencing them – all
the way through.' Fear is real and often entirely justified, but fear
doesn't have to have the final word if we dare to trust in God.

Now, this could sound glib. I suspect Isaiah felt that a little when
constantly inviting the people not to be afraid when all sorts of
complicated threats faced them in the future as well as the present.
I wonder if Jesus, who often told his friends not to be afraid, sometimes thought twice before saying it. Consider his distraught and
bereaved friend Mary Magdalene. She visits a tomb expecting to see
a corpse and finds an empty shroud; then, to make matters worse,

an angel tells her not to be afraid. What would I do in those circumstances? I think I would be more than a little scared – and rightly so.

Isaiah is a complete realist. The exiles will only be able to trust the comfortable words if they can also trust that the hard words aren't spared. This is real-world stuff and prophets tell the truth.

Fear is real, natural and often appropriate but, as we have seen, it doesn't have to win over us. Like Mary Magdalene in the garden, we might hear whispered, through the fear and confusion of loss, the haunting sound of our name, being called to dare to wait for a new future in which fear might be embarrassed by the merest hint of world-defying joy.

God, who sent his Son into the real world and didn't exempt him from fear and pain, strengthen us to face the world without fear and open our ears to hear the haunting melody of defiant joy. Amen.

WEEK 3: TUESDAY

Name games (43.1)

I have called you by name.

Names matter. In some parts of the world your name represents more than a distinguishing identity marker – it captures your character. I remember my youngest son bringing home a school friend in London – a great lad who came from Nigeria. Over a meal one day, I asked him what his full name was – we knew him only as Temi. That was a mistake. He had 15 names because all his family offered him names when he was a baby and these names expressed hopes, aspirations, prayers and insights into the person he might be or become. We just stuck with Temi.

In the Western world, names have largely become labels, devoid of significance (unless you happen to be named after a pop star or footballer, of course). My in-laws once gave me a paperweight for Christmas and through the heavy glass I could read a definition of the name Nicholas: something about 'winner of great victories', which I took to be a joke.

Yet names in the Bible are more like Nigerian names – full of meaning and significance. Isaac was named following his mother's response to the news that she would give birth in old age – it means 'laughter' – and proved that God can handle us laughing at his surprising news. Jesus – Yeshua – speaks of saving his people. Peter is the rock on which Jesus says he will build his church – probably to the chagrin of the other disciples, who know how impetuous and flaky he can be. Luke tells the story of a woman who is the laughing stock of the village, unclean and ostracized, until Jesus heals her from decades of illness and social isolation. He looks at the religious leaders, who specialize in missing the point, and refers to the woman as 'a daughter of Abraham', thereby immediately restoring to her an identity, a history, a community and a dignity she had thought gone for ever (Luke 13.10–17).

It gets even better. We keep coming across people in the biblical story who have their names changed following an encounter with God in some way or other. The obvious example is, again, Peter, who began life as Simon. When, at Caesarea Philippi, Jesus puts him on the spot and asks him to declare his hand regarding Jesus' identity ('Who do *you* say that I am?' (Matthew 16.15)), Jesus then announces that he is changing his name to Peter (Cephas, Petros, the rock). In doing so, Jesus is seeing what this man might become once he has passed through the waters and the fire and found himself stripped of his pretensions. It seems Jesus understood that the rock might be more limestone than granite.

This is surely hopeful for those of us who constantly feel like frauds – or who assume that God only calls those who have got their lives and theology entirely together. It seems that we are known by our names and God even has the ability to change our names in order to promise that the potential he sees will be fulfilled. All this while limestone gets shaped by the elements.

This brings us back to the exiles and the promise Isaiah articulates to them. 'I have known you by name', says God. The name of his people indicates who God thinks they are and who they might become. The bottom line, of course, is that they should in their name bear witness to the name of God. This means that there should be some consistency between the character of God and the visible character of those who bear his name. In the Lord's Prayer, 'hallowed be your name' points us not to a label *about* God, but to the character *of* the God to whom we pray and in whom we trust. When Jesus refers to 'in my name' in relation to prayer, for example, he is not saying that the mere utterance of his name guarantees a desired outcome; rather, he is saying: learn to pray and desire and want those things that are consistent with my character . . . which is consistent with the character of the Father.

This is more important and significant than we sometimes realize. God reveals his character as one of self-giving, self-denial, sacrificial, generous, engaging with the world and not exempting himself from it. If we take the character of God even half seriously, then we will realize that praying for our own self-promotion, material accumulation or self-protection at all costs is to pray in a name that is not God's. To take God's name in vain, as the commandment tells us is forbidden, is not primarily to swear or blaspheme; rather, it is to speak or act in such a way as to deny the character of God and therefore bear witness to some other idol.

To be known by name brings both massive blessing and reassurance on the one hand but also great responsibility on the other. If it is all right for Sarai (whose name is changed to Sarah in the light of Isaac's imminent arrival) to laugh at or with God, then that part of his character is also to be taken as something to be embraced by those who bear his name.

God of Sarah, Isaac, Peter and the 'daughter of Abraham', help us to hear our names on your lips and grant us the power to own your name in our living and speaking. Amen.

WEEK 3: WEDNESDAY

Losing my religion (48.10)

Tested . . . in the furnace of adversity.

There are many reasons why people lose their faith. Some become disillusioned by the Church, others conclude that there is no God. Among all possible reasons, however, by far the most common (in my experience) seems to be some sort of unresolved trauma, loss or suffering.

One of literature's most famous examples of this is to be found in Dostoyevsky's *The Brothers Karamazov*. In a very long book that follows the lives of three brothers and their father, one of them, Ivan, cannot reconcile human suffering with the notion of a personal and benevolent God. He tells his brother a parable about Christ returning and being imprisoned by the Grand Inquisitor, who banishes Jesus from Earth because he believes it is a brutal burden to have given human beings freedom.

Stephen Fry famously repudiated any notion of God on the grounds that the existence of a parasitic worm that does unspeakable things to an eyeball must negate such an idea. It is hard not to sympathize.

But it isn't as easy as that. When people lose their faith, it is important to understand what faith it is they have lost. If faith is in a God who must intervene in any situation of danger or inconvenience in order to preserve me from harm, what sort of God would this be? A world in which the laws of physics are constantly broken would not be a world in which anyone could live anyway. When people lose their faith because, for example, an elderly parent has died, it raises questions about our fundamental acceptance of human mortality.

This might sound harsh but sometimes we need to lose the magical object of a vague religion in order to clear the space for discovering the God who, rather than exempting himself from human mortality, opts into the world at Christmas and sees it through to Calvary and beyond.

This goes to the heart not only of Christian faith but also that of the exiles, whose experience we are exploring here. As we have already seen, every day they woke up, they saw evidence of their own apparent religious delusion. Sitting by the rivers of Babylon, subjected to the mockery of their captors, their experience told them that either the God of the cosmos had deserted them or had been defeated by small tribal gods or never existed in the first place. So what kept them going?

The thing about faith is that it won't always let you go. The rumour of God has a habit of hanging around even when we have lost all our other bearings. The exiles kept alive the songs of home and thereby found themselves haunted by the melodies and language of a place where they belonged more truly than in Babylon. Empires come and go but 'home' remains rooted in the soul. As the psalmist reflects, 'Where can I go from your spirit? Or where can I flee from your presence? . . . I come to the end – I am still with you' (Psalm 139.7, 18).

This has always been true of God's people. Suffering, exile, exposure to all that the world can throw at them – all these are common experiences for those who inhabit this contingent Earth and find themselves hearing the whispered echoes of another world. Yet, like Paul in the New Testament, they have to develop resilience and learn to endure through suffering. How and why? Because the primary vocation of God's people throughout the biblical story is to bear witness to a God who is faithful to us and who invites us to be faithful to him . . . whatever the circumstances. Ridiculous? Yes, in one sense; but exactly what Jesus himself did in (as Matthew puts it in 5.17) 'fulfilling' the vocation of Israel ('the law and the prophets').

This might help us to lose our fear of losing our religion. If our religion reduces God to a personal deity whose job it is to keep us safe and sound in a mucky and threatening world, we simply will not cope with real life and all that the world can throw at us. God has to be set free to draw us into the heart of the real world, not exempting us from that world but promising to stick with us, drawing us by hope and dispelling our fear. Perhaps we have to lose our illusions about God before we can see him as he truly is.

The flip side of this is that, perhaps bizarrely, when we lose our grasp of God, he doesn't lose his grasp of us. Perhaps, when we lose our faith in God – maybe because our belief was misguided or our experience too brutal – God does not lose his faith in us. The exiles will almost certainly have included those who wanted to give up on Yahweh and try out the more successful gods of their captors. Others will have wobbled in doubt about God's reality or faithfulness or their own ability to stay true to their vocation. Others still will have stood in judgement on the wobblers, damning them for their feebleness in faith, but Isaiah makes it clear that the apparent silence of God does not equal the absence of God. Exile will not have the final word.

The Roman Catholic composer James Macmillan wrote of the Japanese novelist Shusaku Endo's experience of the silence of God:

> [God's] silence is not absence, but presence. It is the silence
> of accompaniment rather than nihil. . . . It is a shocking
> reminder that God's power is not of this place, but something
> other. It is presence as absence; absence as presence; which is
> precisely what music is.
> ('Divine Accompaniment', *The Guardian*, 19 August 2003)

**God, whose voice we long to hear and whose presence we yearn
to discern, grant us the patience to endure, the sensitivity to**

hear your haunting whisper of love and the bloody-mindedness to keep hanging on in there. Amen.

WEEK 3: THURSDAY

Losing our memory (44.21; 49.4)

Remember these things.

I remember seeing a television documentary about a musician who had completely lost his memory. He spent his day writing down everything he did and everybody he met. After a few minutes, he had no recollection of who people were or what he had just done. It was heart-rending to see him greet his wife as if he had never met her before.

Memory is more than the simple ability to recall people, facts or events. Memory is integral to identity. We know who we are – partly – in relation to where we have come from. It is not merely a truism that we can't know who we are if we don't know where we have come from, and can't know where we are going if we don't know who and where we are now. Memory matters.

It doesn't just matter to us as individuals. Nations and communities create narratives based on their common memory and that is not always positive. For example, it is over 300 years since King William crossed the Boyne in Ireland (1690) and the people are still divided – re-enacting every year those shaped memories that keep the wounds fresh.

The danger is selecting those elements of history that justify our collective behaviour now. On a visit to Virginia once, I was surprised to hear people talking about 'the recent unpleasantness', referring to the American Civil War. (It was also referred to as 'the Lost Cause' and 'the War of Northern Aggression'.) The language itself tells a story. The danger is that we write the 'history' in order to create a 'memory' that justifies our (usually bad) behaviour now – especially in relation to those who inconveniently share 'our space'.

Isaiah's exiles face a similar challenge, one that is easily recognizable to us in a different world. Who are we when the God who gives us identity appears to have disappeared? If we are not Yahweh's people, then to whom do we owe our existence and our destiny? What is the narrative that gives us place and meaning?

This was not a new question for the exiles. Their whole tradition was shaped around stories and rituals that ensured they should not forget their story. Go back to the exodus when the people were delivered from over four hundred years of captivity and oppression as an immigrant community in a strange land. As their 40-year sojourn in the desert draws towards its conclusion and the people prepare to enter the land of promise, they are given a load of instructions about how they must order their common life in the future. For example, they are to celebrate annual festivals that will involve their bodies, minds and spirits in retelling and reliving the story of their liberation. Why? Because God knows how quickly human beings forget – how easily and effortlessly we lose the plot.

A good example is found in the Festival of the First Fruits in Deuteronomy 26. The first 10 per cent of your crop is to be brought and laid at the feet of the priest. Your reward is to recite a creed – the oldest form of creedal statement in the Bible, beginning 'My father was a wandering Aramean ...' (Deuteronomy 26.5, NIV). The idea behind it is: when you get into the land of promise, you will settle down and build your homes and businesses and it won't be long before you forget that you were once slaves and couldn't save yourselves ... and you will begin to treat other people like slaves. So, at points through the year, you will remind yourselves in word and costly action that you belong to a community that knows its need of God and each other.

At Passover, Jewish children ask the questions that cause their parents' and grandparents' generation to retell the story that says who they actually are. In the Christian Eucharist (Communion), we move from confession of our need of God's grace . . . through hearing the Word of the Lord . . . through bringing our prayers for the world and ourselves . . . through the conflict-healing Peace . . . to the retelling of the Christian story in the Eucharistic Prayer. Here we re-member our story, putting back together the elements of the events that remind us who Christians are: rooted in the life, death, resurrection, ascension of Jesus and the sending of the Holy Spirit to empower his people to live in a Christlike way now.

So it is important that we pay attention to what story we tell and how we tell it. A German academic friend of mine, Dr Isolde Karle, once said at a conference:

> This [Christian] cultural memory cannot be taken for granted. It is completely imaginable that one day the story of the Good Samaritan will no longer be known/understood. Solidarity with the powerless, deliberate care of the marginalized, of the sick and of people in need are not self-evident.

I think she is right.

Lord, forgive our amnesia and help us to remember our story, which is your story, that, dependent on your grace, we might live graciously with others. Amen.

WEEK 3: FRIDAY

Newness after loss (48.6)

I make you hear new things.

How are we to hear new things when the old things reverberate so loudly in our heads?

One of the biggest challenges for many people is being able to hear good news when their senses and consciousness are constantly bombarded with bad news. People who have suffered as children sometimes find it difficult to believe that the good news they hear is actually for them. How can I believe I am loved when all I have experienced is abuse, exploitation or neglect? No wonder that genuine offers of love or affection can be met with suspicion or rejection.

If individuals struggle with this experience, then so do communities. The exiles have had several generations of bad news – as we have seen, they open their eyes and ears every day to evidence of divine neglect, absence or silence. No doubt there were those among their company who wanted to force a return from exile; others would just want a quiet life to continue for as long as possible; still others would wallow in their fatalistic misery and not spot the light penetrating the darkness. Something psychotherapists speak of is the difficulty some people have leaving the darkness behind – a bit like the prisoners who find the cell door opened but don't want to walk through it to freedom because the present pain or misery is more comfortable (and less threatening) than the uncertainties and obligations that lie beyond.

So, rather than colluding in the misery, how does the prophet enable this mixed group of people to hear good news – or, at least, new things?

Or, to refer back to an image from Week 1, how, when we find ourselves in the dried-up space of the desert, are we to look for the flowers that grow only in the desert? If our eyes are accustomed only to see certain things, then how do we force them to 'look' differently? Maybe we need someone else to come alongside us and patiently turn our attention to what we otherwise filter out of view. Maybe we need someone to keep pointing us towards a different possibility – speaking a language of hope and love and colour when all we are used to is words of criticism, blandness or the closing down of potential.

I think this is what is going on here with the exiles. It is easy to read the text and wonder what the problem was – why they didn't just snap out of it and brighten up. But imagine yourself into their experience again. The future looks closed because that future cannot be imagined without a will that looks to some others like fantasy or romanticism.

The exiles would have been familiar with the story captured in Genesis 4 about Cain and Abel. Cain kills his brother and is expelled from the land and his family/community. We read that he settled in the land of Nod and built a city he called Enoch. How odd. Why did he do that and what does it mean? In 1962, a French jurist and theologian called Jacques Ellul wrote an eye-opening book called *The Meaning of the City*. He describes how Cain is enacting a parable of human beings, at sea in a vast expanse of uncontoured meaninglessness, creating a place in which they make meaning and know who they are in relation to others. So we build defensive walls that create a smaller universe than the vast one in which we are so miniscule and transient.

The question I asked in my book *Hungry for Hope* took this one step further. What happens when the carefully constructed, personal world of meaning is breached – usually by trauma or loss? We face a choice: rebuild the damaged wall even thicker so it won't be breached again . . . or dare to look outside the walls and venture out into the unknown, confident only that if God is God of my little universe, then he must be God of all the rest too.

That is the choice and the promise facing Isaiah's exiles. Are you open to hearing new things and moving eventually into a new world or are you more comfortable staying where you are? The new things are not actually new, as the 'story' of God and his people has not changed since the beginning, but to embrace new ways of being – even in old places that are not as they were in the past and must therefore be now new – will involve choice and the taking of responsibility for that choice.

Look through the Bible and this truth is always there. Bartimaeus (Mark 10.46–52) is blind and complaining. However, when Jesus, through his friends, invites him to 'Take heart; get up, he is calling you', Bartimaeus has to decide whether to sit in his familiar place or get up and take his place in the community of Jesus' followers and his wider society.

The first thing is to be open to hearing new things.

Lord, who gives sight to the blind and opens the ears of the deaf, strengthen us by your Spirit that we might have the courage to hear new things, leave the familiar ways and take on new responsibilities for the sake of your Son. Amen.

WEEK 3: SATURDAY

Speaking of faith (48.6)

Will you not declare it?

Charles Wesley once said that we learn our theology not from what we hear from the pulpit but from what we sing. Put an idea or narrative to music and it gets into our heads more firmly than it would if just spoken or read or heard. Of course, the other element is that when we sing, we are being active and committed to more than vague thoughts.

Isaiah's message is coming to a point where hearing the words of comfort or challenge, of encouragement or warning, is not enough. He tells the people that they have to become proclaimers of the truth they have experienced or encountered – articulators of hope, not simply consumers of optimism: 'You have heard; now see all this; and will you not declare it?' (48.6).

The thing about faith is that it has to be spoken and enacted, not just believed. Indeed, 'belief' for the Hebrews involved body, mind and spirit. As we noted in Mark 1.14–15, 'believe in the good news' meant 'commit yourself – body, mind and spirit – to what you now see differently (of God's presence in the world while everything remains tough for you)'. Faith is never just a sort of intellectual assent to a set of propositions about God; rather, it involves the assertion of the will in committing to a way of life that is rooted in the character of God as revealed in Jesus Christ.

This also involves articulating the faith. One of the odder elements of contemporary Christianity is the lack of confidence in speaking of God in credible ways to a sceptical secular society that assumes religion to be a private entertainment anyway. When creating the Diocese of Leeds in 2014, the vision I framed was not exciting, but reflected what had always been the vocation of the Church:

> to be a vibrant diocese (that is, vibrating between the wind of the Spirit and the wind of the world – caught in the tension between them), equipping confident clergy to enable confident Christians to live and tell the good news of Jesus Christ in our region.

Not everybody liked it (and no one offered an alternative), but it was a starter for ten. I included 'tell the good news' precisely because we Christians have to get better at more naturally speaking of God in the public square (which includes anywhere outside a church building).

Again, not everyone was happy with my dismissal of St Francis of Assisi's alleged instruction to his friars: 'Go and preach the gospel. Use words if you have to.' There is no evidence he ever said this – and if he did, he was wrong. We talk about everything else in the pub and on the bus, so why be shy about God? Why the lack of confidence?

Well, there might be many answers to this question but Christians can't avoid the challenge to declare the new things God is doing. This is no different from the challenge to Isaiah's exiles all those years ago. They are living in a hostile environment in which they are mocked for their trust in a God who appears not to be there. They risk ridicule every time they open their mouths or sing their songs. They live in a polytheistic region where deities are tribal and evidence of their power matters. Now they are being asked to believe in a future (liberation) that they can neither see nor envisage from where they currently sit. Not only are they to talk to each other and keep alive the language of home but they are also being asked to articulate the prophet's 'redescription of reality' (Walter Brueggemann, 2009) before a sceptical world. Does this sound familiar?

The point is that God's people are called in every generation to acknowledge the apparent 'evidence' of the world around them and then proclaim the new things of God anyway. Faith has never been any different. As Isaiah makes clear to his people in his day, however, such faith is placed not in a formula but in the person of God. This matters enormously. If faith is dependent on God sorting out my problems, delivering me from the 'slings and arrows of outrageous fortune', then that faith will not survive for long (unless it pushes into reality-denying fantasy).

I was once asked in a national radio interview what happens when we die. I replied that I don't care. The interviewer looked surprised and said, 'Well, don't you think you should care, given your job?' (I was Bishop of Croydon at the time.) My answer was simple: Christian faith is rooted in the person of God, who raised Christ from the dead. I trust in him and the rest is detail. In other words, arguments about what happens after death (and in which order) might be entertaining or even distracting, but they miss the point that our faith is in God and not some schedule.

'Will you not declare it?' asks the prophet. A cellar was discovered in Cologne, Germany, where Jews had been hidden in 1942. On the wall was scrawled the following: 'I believe in the sun though it is late in rising. I believe in love though it is absent. I believe in God though he is silent.' That is what it looks like to articulate the faith of Isaiah.

Lord, our mouths too easily become frozen and our hearts lose courage to speak of you. Give us, by your Spirit, the gift of confidence to declare the newness you promise. Amen.

Week 4: Power and faithfulness

WEEK 4: SUNDAY

Introduction to the week

Even if adults have sometimes lost the excitement of Advent and the building of the story and our expectations, children generally can't contain it. It might be for the wrong reasons, of course, but it is hard to live with the anticipation of Advent in the run-up to Christmas – especially as it is dominated by the more materialistic drive of the media and advertising. We want to skip to the big day without making the journey to it. As we noted earlier, Advent offers us the opportunity to step back, pause a while and live with a retelling of the story of God and his people.

This, though, is hard to do. We know what is coming: Jesus will be born and the angels will sing for joy, but we also have to try to live with the expectation and anticipation, knowing the end of this part of the story while consciously living as if we don't know what is to come. The effort is very worthwhile – delayed gratification and all that – but Advent poses another challenge beyond the mere waiting.

When Andrew Lloyd Webber was planning his television search for someone to play Jesus in a stage revival of *Jesus Christ Superstar*, the obvious question was, what sort of Jesus are you looking for? Is it a controllable and tame Jesus, with beautifully blow-dried hair, treading kindly and ineffectually through a world that doesn't touch him? Is it a macho Jesus who draws women to look after him while proving himself to be stronger than all the other alpha males around him? Is it some other sort of Jesus? There is no neutral Jesus on offer.

This is the question we have to wrestle with as we dare to question our own assumptions in the final week before Christmas explodes in the cry of the tiny babe in Bethlehem. Do we shape Jesus into our own image – one with which we are comfortable and one we can control – or can we look again and allow our own assumptions and expectations to be exposed and challenged?

WEEK 4: MONDAY

The Servant? (42.1)

Here is my servant.

How we understand certain well-known bits of the Bible depends on how we read them.

For example, one of the most repeated statements around the crucifixion narrative is the exclamation by the centurion who has watched Jesus die: 'Truly this man was God's Son!' (Matthew 27.54). Another translation (NIV) puts it like this: 'Surely he was the Son of God!' Other translations are variations on a theme. Given that the Greek has no capital letters and no punctuation, this means that the translator has to frame the words in some way or other and this will involve making assumptions about how the phrase was spoken originally. What if, as Tom Wright has suggested and I have often wondered, the centurion was echoing the scepticism of his people and, looking at the bloodied failure hanging on the gallows, was asking the question sarcastically: 'Really? *This* was the Son of God?!' – the unspoken next question being, 'Are you serious? *Him*?'

On our journey through Advent in the company of Isaiah and his exiles, we have noted the challenge of seeing a future when the present looks terminal – of daring to hope when those around you accuse you of indulging in wishful thinking or some delusionary form of self-comforting fantasy. We have tried to imagine ourselves into the experience of those who have to take time to rethink what it looks like for God to be present with them – not only when all their problems are resolved but even while they suspect he has absented himself from them. Now we come to the point where the good news of liberation is focused in the person of God's Servant but the exiles are asked what this Servant might look like. How are they to recognize the Servant (which is Israel herself in her true vocation) when they might be looking out for one who looks different? Will they miss the flower that grows only in the desert while looking for others?

When Isaiah introduces the Servant in chapter 42, he does so having had a bit of a laugh about idols and the futility of worshipping or serving small gods. The introduction to the Servant is remarkable in that he, imaging the God he serves, does not exist for the sake of his own power or well-being but for the sake of the world . . . and, more to the point, for all the 'wrong' people. If you assume that poor and downtrodden people only have themselves (or their naughty parents) to blame for their predicament, how would it sound when we hear that God's liberating agent 'in whom my soul delights' will quietly 'bring forth justice', refusing to break a 'bruised reed' or 'quench a dimly burning wick'? This is hardly the stuff of mighty deities, whose job it is to exercise power and bless the powerful.

Yet here Isaiah is clear: Israel's God is the God who 'created the heavens and stretched them out, who spread out the earth and what comes from it, who gives breath to the people upon it and spirit to those who walk in it' (42.5). The Creator of the cosmos (not a mere tribal deity) is one who, surprisingly and maybe even shockingly, gives himself to and for the world, paying particular attention to those who have become victims of that world. In the ancient Middle East that was decidedly weird.

Reading this, we also hear echoes of what Jesus will say when he begins his public ministry and reads from Isaiah in his home town synagogue (Luke 4.14–30):

The Servant? (42.1)

The Spirit of the Lord is upon me, because he has anointed me to bring good news to the poor. He has sent me to proclaim release to the captives and recovery of sight to the blind, to let the oppressed go free, to proclaim the year of the Lord's favour.
(Luke 4.18–19)

Jesus rolls up the scroll, looks the people in the eye and brazenly claims that this is now being fulfilled in himself. No wonder they tried to push him off a cliff. The arrogance of it.

When I imagine myself into that place – either standing alongside the exiles in their misery or the people trying to hear the word of the Lord in the synagogue in Nazareth – I can feel the caution, the shock and the outrage. I am naturally cautious by nature, a late developer rather than an early adopter (to use contemporary language). It is hard to dislodge a firm impression or a deeply held (if not critically appraised) conviction about God or his character when faced with a new perspective or claim. I would probably have been with the outraged.

However, the other surprising thing about Isaiah's revelation of the nature of this Servant is that he is not just on the side of his own people; rather, he will bring forth justice to *the nations*. This should not be surprising; but it comes to a people who are having to be reminded of their fundamental story: that the primary vocation of Israel had always been, from creation in the 'image of God' (and the so-called 'cultural mandate') in Genesis and through the calling of the patriarchs to the exodus into a new world and a new society, one of service – laying down their lives in order that the world might see who God is and what God is about. The vision of the Servant as Isaiah expresses it is only surprising or shocking because this vocation had been so thoroughly lost. The implication is that exile was a necessary and inevitable means of giving the time and space for Israel to lose their illusions about God and themselves in order to clear the way for a recovery of that vocation.

God, who has always called your people to give their lives for the sake of the world, forgive us our forgetfulness and set us free to recognize your Servant afresh – and then to follow his way in our time and place. Amen.

WEEK 4: TUESDAY

Justice and covenant (42.3)

He will faithfully bring forth justice.

When we read about God being 'faithful', what do we think this faithfulness actually looks like? Does it mean that God is promising to be faithful to his people and for them to trust in his vindication of them and their cause? Does it refer to God's faithfulness to his own nature and will – or something else?

Yesterday we saw that this God sees beyond his own people and locates himself and his will in the context of the whole world: 'he will bring forth justice to the nations'. Presumably, this also includes the oppressive Babylonians, who have been keeping the Israelites captive. Justice cannot be simply for those who want to see themselves vindicated over against everyone else. Justice has to transcend particular interests or it is not justice.

The prophets make abundantly clear that justice lies at the heart of God's character and is primarily measured by how the powerful and powerless are treated in society. As a poet once observed, if you don't have justice, you're left with just ice. The point is well made: it is a cold world where justice is a commodity to be bought and sold or where lip service is paid to human dignity and justice has become a means of privilege to those who either are powerful or have the skill or means to manipulate it for their own ends and in their own interests.

Yet justice is not merely functional – essential to the good ordering of human society and life together. Dostoyevsky once wrote to Katkov (a contemporary Russian nationalist; Mochulsky, 1971, pp. 272–3): 'Juridical punishment for crime scares a criminal far less than law-makers think, partly because the criminal himself requires it morally.' In other words, justice isn't simply about keeping the peace and good order – deterring the wrongdoers – or fulfilling a bureaucratic demand in order to keep elected politicians happy with their harshness. Rather, Dostoyevsky here appeals to something far more fundamental: criminals require justice because only this takes seriously their humanity, their moral accountability, their very being as moral agents who have both rights and responsibilities in a human community of mutual obligation.

So when we read in Isaiah 42 that God will 'faithfully' bring forth justice to the nations, we are reading something utterly consistent with the whole biblical narrative. God has chosen his people to be those who live out God's justice in and for the wider world – regardless of whether they themselves benefit or suffer from this in their common life. But if God's people forget this vocation and prioritize their own sense of justice (or entitlement) over that of others, then the faithful God of justice will not defend them from the consequences of their heresy. What we read in Isaiah is the outworking of that theological amnesia.

Remember, though, that it is into this situation that Isaiah brings word of God's faithfulness. Liberation is coming because death, violence, destruction and corruption do not and will not have the final word in a world that has God's character at its heart.

This poses a question for the contemporary Church that haunts me and to which I have not yet found an answer. When I think about or talk about the Church in the United Kingdom today – its mission, challenges and opportunities – which part of the biblical narrative do I unconsciously assume to be the locus of its language? Walter Brueggemann, for instance, suggests that the Church in the West is in exile; and the way that the Church behaves, speaks, listens and hears in exile is not the same as when it is basking in the abundant blessing of the Promised Land. I will polarize to make the point.

The task of the exiles is to keep alive the language and songs of home while in a foreign land. This is not the time – decades and sometimes centuries – when miracles happen and the people of God expand and grow; it is a time for hanging on and just keeping the rumours of God alive. At the other extreme, however, if we assume that the Church of today is in the Promised Land, growing our harvests and building our future, seeing fruitfulness and expansion everywhere (and attributing this to the favour of our God), we will use different language and apply different models to our common Christian life. So where are we today? And what are the implications of our answer to the question?

This is not a trivial question, but it brings us back to the nature of God in all times as the one who will bring forth justice regardless of who suffers if justice is ignored. It is a perpetual danger for the people of God that they forget their primary vocation and see justice as serving their own interests and consolidating their own security and identity. We should be bolder.

God of justice, open our eyes to see your world and all people as you see them. Burn in our hearts with the faithfulness that you also require from those who bear your name and claim your favour. Amen.

WEEK 4: WEDNESDAY

Open blind eyes (42.6–7)

A light to the nations, to open the eyes that are blind.

Why do blind eyes need to be opened?

It might seem a rather stupid question. Surely, people who cannot see must want to see? Light is preferable to darkness, isn't it?

Well, let's pause and think about that for a moment. In the daylight, we miss seeing the vast depths of the universes and stars in the night sky. There are things that happen in nature at night that go unspotted during the day. I look at things differently in the darkness than in the light – using my eyes and ears differently as I navigate the places and sounds around me. I love the darkness; it offers sights and sounds and gifts and dangers that the daytime hides from me.

Is light always good? I recently heard a preacher suggesting that we all love living in the light and I thought he must be an idealist par excellence. I do like living in the light . . . except when the light exposes the things I would rather not see. I think it was C. S. Lewis who said that our job is not to stare at the light but to see what around us is illuminated by the light. The problem is that when the light is shone on myself and my own failures and weaknesses, I prefer the darkness. Light does not discriminate in what it illuminates, but we can all choose what to look at and what to ignore.

This would have been a powerful reminder to the exiles that they had spent decades unable to hide from what the light exposed in their own vocational amnesia. If the people whose God is the Creator of the cosmos had gone into exile bewildered at this surprisingly negative turn of events, the lack of a quick resolution had by now stripped them of any illusions. They are not in Babylon for fun. They are not being mocked by their captors in some entertaining effort to help them recover their identity. When all is stripped away, you can't avoid the hard questions.

When I was a teenager in Liverpool, I was surrounded by all the self-protecting props of a large church (Baptist), lots of role models, constant theological stimulation and missional activities. Evangelism oozed consciously from everything I did (causing me now some excruciating memories). Then, in my second year as a student of German and French, I went out to a small town in southern Germany to do a placement as a freelance technical translator. I was unwell, lonely, miserable and, probably, depressed. I had never experienced anything like it and it was utterly debilitating. I did my work well but, outside work (and inside my head and heart), I was in a very dark place. There were days when I got the bus back from the village where my boss's office was and went straight to bed – just in order to close my mind and exclude the misery and loneliness.

There, in Schwäbisch Gmünd, I could no longer avoid the hard questions about God's reality or the truthfulness of the Christian faith. Things I assumed and had taken for granted fell apart. Was God even there? How do I account for love and meaning – especially when God seems at worst absent or at best silent? I felt derelict. Whether I liked it or not, I had to start again and rebuild a credible Christian faith that made sense in and related to the real world. It was the beginning of a long (and continuing) journey of faith and resistance, often testing and frustrating, sometimes joyful, always surprising.

I think this is a bit like the experience of the exiles. The point is that the light is not always comfortable or welcome, even if, in time, it proves to be the thing that forces us to open our eyes and see more clearly – whatever truth we then find ourselves exposed to. The key, of course, is not to blind ourselves again in order to retain the security of the darkness.

When Jesus begins his public ministry and reads from Isaiah (Luke 4) or sets out his purpose (Mark 1.14–15), he promises to fulfil the calling of Israel to open the eyes of the blind. Then we see him do it – making the 'kingdom of God' real and demonstrating that God is present among his people in a way that goes against their assumptions. How do we know that the vocation of the Servant is being embodied in him? Well, we see the blind having their eyes opened, but opened to what?

Let's not be romantic about the healings in the Gospels. When, in Mark 10, blind Bartimaeus hears that great invitation from the friends of Jesus – 'Take heart. Get up. He is calling *you*' – he faces a choice. He could stay with the familiarity of the road and his dependency on the reluctant charity of others. To get up and approach Jesus might bring changes that he doesn't want. Wanting to see is one thing; taking the responsibilities that come with being a seeing person (including, in his society, working for a living and giving alms to the blind) might be more challenging.

We might be people who welcome having our eyes opened to the grace and mercy of God in Jesus Christ. We might be people who, having heard nothing but bad news about ourselves and the world we live in, rejoice in seeing ourselves as God sees us. We might be people who have only opened our eyes slightly and need encouragement to let the long-dimmed light gradually expose them to the reality of the world and of God. Whatever the case, the healing of our blindnesses will bring challenge as well as freedom, responsibility as well as liberation and pain as well as joy.

God of light and liberation, open our eyes to see your face, that we might see as we are seen and, in the freedom of this light, we might open the eyes of others to your love and grace. Amen.

WEEK 4: THURSDAY

No hiding place (50.6)

I did not hide my face.

If we were asked to describe a superhero, a champion of the people, a liberator, I suspect most of us would come up with someone powerful, muscular, smart and unflinchingly fearless. I further suspect that when most people of Isaiah's day thought about the promised messiah, they would almost certainly have envisaged someone of a similar ilk.

I know it is a hard exercise, but try to imagine being among the people who, unconsciously expecting such a leader, are suddenly presented with someone who doesn't conform to that picture they had in their heads. Here we are back to the earlier references to Andrew Lloyd Webber's search for a television Jesus (for the *Jesus Christ Superstar* revival) and that curious question: what sort of a Jesus are you looking for? Is it the macho rescuer of people? Is it the wimp in the white nightie with billowing waves in his hair and a smile on his pale, Caucasian face? Something else? The writer Jeanette Winterson bemoans the fact that 'Jesus, the iconoclast, outlaw, and liberator, without possessions or allegiances, is so uncomfortable for the Church, that while his name is constantly invoked, his radicalism is ignored' (in a review of *Doubts and Loves* by Richard Holloway, *The Times*, 19 September 2001).

Then this person appears as a Servant who 'did not hide his face'. We have a choice at this point: either we keep looking for the messiah who will conform to what we want to see or we rethink our prejudice about what a messiah should look and sound like and say and do. This is not an easy choice: the former maintains security (in a funny sort of way) whereas the latter shakes your world up and leaves everything open to surprise (which might be good or bad). The former demands a closed mind; the latter invites courage.

What is clear is that the image of the Servant (not the Leader) comes as a bit of a shock. How is someone who is victimized, beaten and scarred going to be of any use in setting people free? Which of our enemies is going to be impressed by such a feeble opponent?

Well, Isaiah's exiles might have preferred a different type of messiah, in the same way that many were looking for a better kind of saviour than what they saw in Jesus of Nazareth. If the exiles were mocked for, as they saw it, serving a useless God who had left them defeated, homeless and singing songs by the rivers of Babylon, how much more must the friends of Jesus have felt this when they saw their 'hopes and dreams' bleeding on a cross?

The shock of this is something we too easily either sanitize or forget. You look for a strong liberator, only to find a Servant with a challenging manifesto (look again at chapters 42 and 49) who then turns out, from chapter 50 onwards, to look a bit feeble: 'I did not turn backwards. I gave my back to those who struck me, and my cheeks to those who pulled out the beard; I did not hide my face from insult and spitting' (50.5–6).

However, this is the key. The people of God are always asked to be open to surprise by a God who, in the words of the Old Testament theologian Walter Brueggemann (2009), 'redescribes reality'. It is a servant and not a leader who comes to God's people and invites them to look at God and the world differently. This Servant, rather than fighting harder than the other powers, offers them his back and his face and defuses their fire by not running away. This God does things differently, offering what looks like weakness ,but turning it into power – the power of a baby in a manger and a man hanging on a cross.

This takes us to the heart not only of Isaiah's exiles but also to that of Advent. What sort of Christ are we looking for as Christmas approaches? Will we recognize the presence of God in the baby of Bethlehem and the child of Nazareth or will we miss him because we expected something a little more robust?

The story of the Bible is of a God who calls a people to bear his name – that is, to look and sound and behave like the God they claim to serve. Though they get it wrong a million times, they are called to lay down their lives in order that the wider world might see and know who God is and what God is about. They are to be un-afraid of apparent weakness and unimpressed by displays of power or strength. For God's way is different. Here it is the mighty who find themselves brought low, while the meek inherit the place of God. It is the losers who find that their mourning is turned into the sort of dancing that the power-merchants find embarrassing.

Christmas will be about God opting into a world of perverted values, thus subverting them in the face of those who think power, beauty and success are ultimate. Here it is all turned on its head. If we want to begin to discover (or reimagine) what this might actually look like, then look for the wounded healer and not the wounding leader.

Lord, open our so easily blinded eyes, that we might see in the face and side and hands of your Servant the real power of God to heal, challenge and love. Amen.

WEEK 4: FRIDAY

Images of love (53.3)

He was despised and rejected.

When I conducted my daughter's wedding, I was struck by the icons of love all around us in the church and at the reception later. Presents and cards were laced with pink or silver love hearts. Romantic, yes; but realistic?

Beauty is a wonderful and mysterious thing. What is it about a beautiful face or a mesmerizing piece of jewellery that captures our attention and holds our gaze? One of the mysteries of our current age is why so many people, visiting a wonderful place, take photographs or video of it on their phones rather than actually look at it and let it be impressed on their memories. To look at something – as part of an holistic experience of 'being there' involving sight, sound, smell and so on – is not the same as to look at it through a mediating lens on a phone. Perhaps this modern technological method of creating memory also manages to keep things at arm's length – at a distance.

So what are Isaiah's exiles to make of the promise of a Servant who is a mess? How credible would a messiah be who is ugly, scarred and a laughing stock among the locals?

Yet here – and made famous again by Handel in his *Messiah* – is the clearest declaration we might find: God's Servant will face rejection, ridicule and deep wounding, and this is the norm, not an aberration. Why?

We need to remember that this text is primarily addressed *to* Israel and *about* Israel – what makes this people special. We then are surprised to discover that people who fulfil the vocation God has given them (to demonstrate to the world who God is and what God is about) will find themselves attacked rather than celebrated. This theme runs through all that follows. Perhaps the obvious illustration of this is to be found in the song Mary sang (Luke 1.46–55) when she discovered she was to give birth (which, in turn, she took from Hannah's song in 1 Samuel 2). I think that if I became pregnant and thought about singing a song, I wouldn't immediately land on something political, but Mary did.

If God has 'scattered the proud in the thoughts of their hearts', this might be good news for the humble objects of other people's pride but it is bad news for the proud. No doubt the news that 'He has brought down the powerful from their thrones, and lifted up the lowly' will be great for the lowly to hear. However, the formerly powerful people will, presumably, not give up without a fight. If God has 'filled the hungry with good things, and sent the rich away empty', that will not be good news to the rich.

Much, much more could be said about the Magnificat and the tradition from which it emerged, but the simple point here is that what we call the gospel – good news – will not be received or experienced as good news by everyone. Those who lose out will not necessarily welcome the bias of God towards the lowly and hungry; Jesus didn't get crucified because he made people feel good about themselves and endorsed the economic or political status quo.

This is harder to address than we sometimes assume. Isaiah's Servant does not come along riding on a war horse, making a noise and threatening to beat people into submission. Rather, he comes as one who serves, who takes what the world throws at him, stays faithful to the nature of the God who sends him and quietly suffers the consequences of this decision to be faithful. This, of course, was always the vocation of God's people – even though they forgot their identity and traded in their humility for hubris and security many times. Jesus of Nazareth comes along (see Matthew 5.17) and claims not to replace or supersede the vocation of Israel but to 'fulfil' it. In other words, we see in Jesus what faithful obedience to the call of God looks like and it isn't some romantic fairy tale that ends happily ever after.

It is one of the ironies of history that people frequently admire those who give up their lives for the sake of the world, while doing everything to ensure their own personal security in it. In October 2018, Pope Francis canonized Archbishop Oscar Romero. Romero spoke out against the men and women (but usually men) of violence in El Salvador during its civil war and, for his pains, was assassinated on 24 March 1980 while celebrating mass. Instead of removing a problem, his death inspired millions and contributed, ultimately, to the downfall of the violent right-wing regime. His statue is one of the ten twentieth-century saints on the west front of Westminster Abbey in London.

It is a paradox that beauty is to be found in people who are despised and rejected, scarred and humiliated. As with resurrection, the last word never goes to the merchants of violence, death and destruction . . . and God will bring sight out of blindness, beauty out of ugliness, hope out of despair.

Lord, in a world that fears humiliation, defeat and rejection, empower your people to be agents of transformation, bringing hope and light where despair and darkness appear to have the final word. Amen.

WEEK 4: SATURDAY

No exemptions (53.11)

Out of his anguish he shall see light.

Suffering must never be trivialized and cannot be romanticized. Suffering is not a mere concept to be debated by philosophers or poets; rather, it is something no person would invite or welcome but everyone will experience in some way or other. To be in the midst of suffering – and not be able to see an end in sight – is dreadful. So, having described the Suffering Servant to the exiles in Babylon, is it not arrogant (or, at least, a cynical fantasy) to speak of 'seeing light' out of 'anguish'?

Well, it would be if it generated some desperate hope that a magic wand would sort out the problem. Anyone who suffers mentally, psychologically, physically or socially can be forgiven for crying out for healing and resolution, but we all know that some forms of suffering will not be alleviated, are not healed and cannot be avoided. The desire for instant change is completely understandable and even laudable – it is a protest against the pain and the injustice that we long to see banished from the world.

But this is tough stuff. We live in a contingent world in which cells replicate and mutate and that, therefore, must allow for cancer. We live in a world where people often prioritize their personal security over faithful obedience to the call of God to be servants and 'a light to the Gentiles'. We live in a world where violence appears to vindicate the 'might is right' brigade and fear is easy to generate. We are not in ultimate control of our own destiny and, despite amazing scientific and technological advances, cannot escape the challenges of mortality and powerlessness in the face of death.

Yet the reason it is not absurd to speak of seeing light out of the anguish of our experience is that, according to Isaiah, the light of God can only be seen from within the real world of human experience. As we have noted several times already, Christmas is about God opting into this precarious material world, with all its beauties, mysteries and horrors, and not exempting himself from it. Hence, his call to his people is to plunge into life in this world, but to decline to see this world as the ultimate end. The kingdom of God – that is, where God is present – is about looking for the light where the darkness claims its reign. As the comedian Frank Skinner observed, 'Faith is a comfort, but it can also be a wound. If it's just like a woolly jumper, it can't be that important, can it?' (Frank Skinner and Archbishop Rowan Williams in conversation, Canterbury Cathedral, 16 September 2011).

The exiles – those longing for home and those who have grown comfortable with their new life – are to look beyond their immediate challenges and be drawn by the (apparently absurd) hope of return. Their imagination as well as their pious devotion is to be orientated towards a future that draws them forwards and shines light on to the path on which their feet are set. Let's look at two perspectives that might help us to understand this.

I was once in Israel with a group of Christian leaders from the UK. We had met people from across the divides of that tiny piece of ground and had heard horror stories of grievance and suffering on all sides. Meeting the Deputy Foreign Minister in his office, we gave him a bit of a hard time. Then, towards the end of our open and frank conversation, he suddenly stood up and banged the conference table around which we were sitting. This is what he said: 'Sometimes it seems as if there is no light at the end of the tunnel. But it is not because the light is not there; it is because the tunnel is not straight.' In other words, caught here in the midst of time and space and not knowing how our situation will develop, we do not and cannot see clearly how things might be resolved one day.

The second illustration comes from an attempt to tweet the meaning and offer of Christian faith at Christmas and Easter, following a radio interview in which I was put on the spot and had to find a pithy phrase to sum it all up. I eventually banged out about 14 phrases that I hoped would shine a different light on an element of Christian faith and truth. One of them was simply: 'Christmas/Easter means being drawn by faith, not driven by fear.' This was the one that took off on social media and ran for days. Christians are not exempt from suffering or empathizing with the suffering of others with whom we share our space in this world. However, we are drawn by the light of a God who beckons us through our anxiety and fear towards a light that does not emanate from our own wishful thinking or fantasy.

Dostoyevsky wrote: 'It is not as a child that I believe and confess Jesus Christ. My hosanna is born of a furnace of doubt.'

In other words, anguish is real and powerful, but it isn't the end and it doesn't have the final word.

This will be seen ultimately in Jesus of Nazareth. The Gospels indicate that he knew the power of fear. Deserted by his friends prior to his arrest and betrayed by those closest to him, he prays that the suffering coming towards him in Jerusalem might be avoided. This was no made-up yarn to make him seem ever so brave under pressure; rather, it is brutally realistic about human fear and the cost of being faithful. Jesus prays and sweats and is desperate for the support of his sleeping friends. Contrary to Eric Idle's song from the cross in Monty Python's *Life of Brian*, the only song to pass his lips, uttered from the depths of agony, was a psalm that expressed the very human sense of having been totally abandoned by God: 'My God, my God, why have you forsaken me?' (Psalm 22.1).

'Out of his anguish he shall see light'; but the anguish will be powerfully real.

Lord, we long to be delivered from suffering and we yearn for security and hope. Root within us that faith which sees light in darkness and dares to offer hope and light to a fearful world. Amen.

Week 5: Joy will find a way

WEEK 5: SUNDAY

Introduction to the week

One of the most perceptive poets and musicians of my generation is the largely unknown Canadian Bruce Cockburn. Back in 1975, he recorded a song about dying, but called it 'Joy will find a way'. He doesn't deny the pain of loss, but is both realistic and hopeful about what can happen through it.

In the song, Cockburn picks up on a biblical theme that constantly surprises us. As we have noted, it is easy to read a psalm or some other text without asking about the context in which it was written – and many psalms were written in circumstances of fear, longing or unresolved uncertainty and suffering. Yet, in all this deeply human experience, joy has a habit of leaking through in unexpected places and ways. Joy cannot be engineered or demanded; rather, it takes us by surprise as we find ourselves sensing that we are not at the end yet – there is more to be said and more to be lived.

An American writer once described the loss of his wife in a book to which he gave the strange title of *A Severe Mercy*. Describing their friendship with C. S. Lewis and conversion to Christianity, Sheldon Vanauken then went on to explore the theme of mercy in a very personal way. In 1985, he published a sequel and called it *Under the Mercy*. It is the titles that grab our attention. Suffering exposes us – when everything else is stripped away – to what ultimately sustains us in our human journey through a messy world: we are held by the mercy of a God who loves us and does not abandon us to hopelessness, whatever our circumstances.

This week, we will see something of what it was like for Isaiah's exiles to sense that they were 'under the mercy' and to hear the whispered promise that, even for them, joy will find a way through and out. As we approach the surprise of Christmas ('God surprising earth with heaven', as John Bell put it) and retell the story in ways that evoke that mystery of the breaking in of God in human flesh in a material world, we do so by singing familiar carols and listening to familiar readings from the Bible. Maybe we also have the opportunity to come at it afresh by accompanying Isaiah's exiles as they are challenged to examine their expectations and limitations and be open to the joy of surprise.

WEEK 5: MONDAY

Sing out! (54.1)

Burst into song and shout.

The leader of the Sojourners Community in the USA, Jim Wallis, described in his great book *The Call to Conversion* how he and his friends were repeatedly arrested for defending the interests of poor people in Washington, DC. He observes that the police just got used to them sitting in the cells and singing – to the extent that, when they got arrested after a period of good behaviour, the police said they had missed the entertainment. Wallis simply draws from this that you just can't stop Christians from singing.

As we have seen, this goes right back to the earliest traditions of Judaism. Songs and poems gave voice to communal experience, personal longings, political grievances and existential musings. As we saw previously, the earliest Hebrew creed (Deuteronomy 26) begins not with some bald statement but a story of a people: 'My father was a wandering Aramean . . .' (Deuteronomy 26.5, NIV). Nearly three thousand years after they were written and collated, the book of Psalms still offers a vocabulary to people who recognize that advances in technology and science do not change one iota the basic human need for identity, value, atonement and love. Lament, praise, complaint, worship, dread, longing, hope and despair: all these find expression in words (and often music) as the poets shape both emotion and rationalization.

To misquote again the great Billy Ocean song, when the going gets tough, the tough write poetry. Even in many of the most desperate psalms, there is some articulation of hope or joy or confidence. Not always – some psalms do not resolve and, if set to music, should always be sung in a minor key – but many reveal that the prison of our misery cannot hold the human spirit for ever. Joy will find a way.

It is interesting that the two most famous biblical characters who resorted to song after hearing surprising news were women. Whereas Sarai, Abram's elderly wife, laughed at the notion that she would give birth to a son through whom the world would be blessed, Hannah and Mary, both of whom probably felt similarly bewildered, are recorded as having burst into song at the news that they were to become pregnant. In fact, as we have seen, Mary's song – known as the Magnificat – derives from Hannah's song.

What is striking about these songs is that they tie justice with joy. They don't burst into some trivial song but into one that is deeply political and powerfully disturbing to those who use their power to dominate powerless and poor people. Clearly, those who hear in these songs that they are going to lose out will not be happy – and their response will probably not be one of joyful acceptance. To those who have grown used to being used, abused, downtrodden or ignored, however, these are songs of joy and hope and justice.

The late poet and musician Leonard Cohen, when introducing a song in his live show, drily observed that he had dug deeply into the religions and had taken a raft of drugs during a long life, 'but joy kept breaking through'. Everyone cheered – I suspect not only at the theatricality of the performance but also the commonality of the experience. Religion doesn't have to be joyless but it often appears to be so, especially if it focuses on what is wrong and negative, sinful and destructive at the expense of hope and redemption, light and good. By the time we have finished reinforcing the effects of sin and evil, we have lost our focus on what God has done about it all. Maybe this is what lies at the heart of the difference between Orthodox churches, which refer in Jerusalem to the 'Church of the Resurrection', and other Western churches, which call it the 'Church of the Holy Sepulchre'.

I sometimes ask myself which song would come out of my heart and mouth (and maybe memory) if I was surprised by joy (as C. S. Lewis describes his conversion and discovery of love through his dying wife, Joy Davidman). What is the theme song that runs through my veins like the word 'Blackpool' through a stick of rock? I can think of many songs from many genres, but I might ultimately come down on 'Joy will find a way' in its emphasis on not giving death and destruction the final word in a difficult world.

Songs are always revealing. They expose the reality of our faith and love and fear. For Isaiah's exiles, they had faithfully kept the songs of 'home' alive while stranded in a foreign land where these songs were mocked. They had hung on to the faith that gave birth to these songs, even when that faith seemed to be absurd and unrealistic, careless of the evidence of their eyes and ears. However, they lived not only in the present – the 'ultimate now', as I have come to speak of it – but also in the expectation that God takes a longer view, new life is possible and a new day will surely dawn. That new day will also bring its own challenges and conflicts, but it will be a new day of opportunity too. That is what provokes joy in the midst of uncertainty.

God, who always promises to surprise his people with joy and who subverts the gloom of the nay-sayers, set our hearts free to sing your songs – and to do so with a defiant and careless joy. Amen.

WEEK 5: TUESDAY

Prophetic action (54.2)

Enlarge the site of your tent.

On Maundy Thursday 2018, Pope Francis knelt before 12 prisoners in the Regina Coeli Prison in Rome. To the dismay of some, who would prefer that he kept this act merely symbolic and confined within the walls of the Vatican, he washed and then kissed the feet of eight Roman Catholics, two Muslims, an Orthodox and a Buddhist. In past years he has done the same to non-Christians and women. Why?

The quick answer is that the Pope believes the gospel of Jesus Christ. For him, leadership means service, but this act of love and mercy to those on the margins of society also demonstrates, in action as well as word, that forgiveness is possible, that Jesus never abandons them, that hope cannot be extinguished. He is also making it clear that the Christian Church must be willing, as Jesus was, to take a risk on people.

In common with many who initiate prophetic acts, not everyone was delighted by his choices.

Think of Rosa Parks refusing to give up her bus seat to a white man in Montgomery, Alabama, on 1 December 1955, prompting Martin Luther King to lead the movement that changed America's racial discrimination laws and cost him his life. When she defied the law – not for the first time but this time running out of patience – she proclaimed to a sceptical world that things needed to change, that human beings are not objects for the fulfilment of other people's prejudices and that enough was enough. She had no assurance that anything would actually change, but she enacted a resistance that revealed to her society a different narrative of how it should be shaped.

Both Rosa Parks and Pope Francis stand in a tradition of prophetic acts that goes back a very long way. It would appear from any reading of the Bible (or a look through history) that God's people are sometimes prompted to do things that might look odd or ridiculous to observers, but serve to make a visible statement of faith or hope. They demonstrate physically that things do not have to be the way they are, the world can change and new beginnings are not only possible but probable.

Think of Jeremiah (in chapter 32), about to be led into exile from his homeland, deciding to buy a field in Anathoth for the future. How absurd! The city is about to fall to the Babylonian forces and you spend good money buying a field that they will occupy for several generations? Yet his was a defiant act of faith in the future – that however bleak the imminent prospects looked, God's people believed in a yet-to-be-imagined future. Jeremiah would not see the fulfilment of this hope, but his children and their children might do. So, in buying a field, he staked a claim for hope; he did something physical and personally costly that challenged the doom-mongers and kept alive a whisper of hope.

It is in this spirit that Isaiah encourages the exiles to 'Enlarge the site of your tent'. Is this not a ridiculous thing to suggest, given that these people have seen their prospects shrink? Yet the enlarging of the site of one's tent implies that more space will be required in this household in the future, that a new flourishing is to begin in the not-so-distant future. In other words, the prophetic action goes beyond words and invokes a visual encounter with embodied faith.

It is also an invitation to go beyond the bounds of previous experience or expectation. An enlarged site creates more space for those who have not belonged here. It makes room for outsiders to be invited into the place of conversation, hospitality and mutuality. An enlarged site suggests openness to a bigger world and the surprise of an enlarged community.

When St Ethelburga's Church in the City of London was seriously damaged by a massive IRA bomb in 1993, it was marked down for demolition. This mediaeval building had survived the Great Fire of

London and the Blitz, so this fate was resisted and the church rebuilt. However, the St Ethelburga's Centre for Reconciliation and Peace inhabited it with a remit to build relationships across divisions of conflict, culture and religion. The building, which included a large tent at its heart, was designed to create a safe space in which difference could be confronted by conversation, enquiry, mutual listening and learning. The site of the tent was enlarged in order that a new way of relating could be tried.

Christmas is pregnant with prophetic acts, from the naming of Jesus and John to the presentation of the Magi's gifts. God comes among us as one of us, getting his hands dirty in the material world and inviting us to put our trust in him – not in a formula for eternal protection, but in the person of God, who shows us who he is and what he is about; in the vulnerability of a baby in a manger in an animals' stall in a small village in an obscure part of the Roman Empire.

God of the future, implant within our imaginations a reckless willingness to live out hope and to act for your kingdom, even where to do so looks ridiculous. Amen.

WEEK 5: WEDNESDAY

Sigh no more (54.4)

You will not be ashamed.

Shame can be a good thing and its loss is seriously damaging to a society. The loss of social sanction for choices, words or actions that diminish human dignity or our common life means more than an absence of blushing.

It doesn't seem so long ago when a politician who lied publicly would find the shame career-ending. Facts mattered and the nature of the public discourse was honoured. Then we got an American President making up 'facts', ignoring reality and lying with such habitual narcissistic frequency that it is like living in Alice's Wonderland (or 1930s Europe). Whatever one thinks about the European Union and the merits of the United Kingdom being part of it, the lies told during the 2016 referendum campaign were breathtaking in their brazenness. Seneca put it like this: 'Shame may restrain what law does not prohibit.' It doesn't always work, though.

The disturbing key to this phenomenon, however, is that, today, those who lie or misrepresent know that it doesn't matter. They will not suffer, nor will their careers or reputations. This is dangerous. A bit of shame might be healthy for our political culture, to say nothing of the example set for our children regarding integrity, honesty and courtesy.

Shame has always functioned as an inhibitor of bad behaviour, perhaps more often because of the social consequences than as the result of moral conscience. Yet, for many individuals, shame is a debilitating wound that inhibits their flourishing as whole people. Shame rooted in guilt eats away over time and diminishes self-worth. That is where the gifts of repentance and forgiveness come in, offering the freedom of a new beginning and a different future.

If we now go back to Isaiah's exiles, we find a people for whom their collective shame is reinforced every waking day as they are mocked by their captors for having such an obviously failed faith. Not only has their God failed them but also they insist on persisting in this fantasy. Their prophets tell them that they are where they are because of their vocational amnesia in the past: they had forgotten their story and how they were to live as God's servant people in a challenging world. And here they now are, ashamed of their past failures to live up to their common calling and ashamed of the humiliation this has caused them.

Now, Rabbi Jonathan Sacks has distinguished between 'shame culture' and 'guilt culture', asserting that Judaism is less concerned with the public judgement of others and more with personal conscience. He concludes: 'What matters is not whether we conform to the culture of the age but whether we do what is good, just and right' (<http://rabbisacks.org/the-power-of-shame-metsorah-5776>). Of course, what happens is that there are social consequences to personal guilt and shame; so both belong together.

Then, Isaiah not only promises his guilt-convicted exiles a bursting into song but also an end to their shame. The promise for the future is that their faith in Yahweh will be vindicated in the end and the watching world will see their return to their home as the end of their humiliation and shame. Isaiah holds out the promise of an end to shame. Their past guilt is not wiped out as if it never happened; their current shame is not going to be simply extinguished. Rather, by facing their guilt and owning their shame, they will one day soon return home with a little more humility and a recognition that, once again, they could not save themselves but needed the grace and severe mercy of God. If they learn from their experience, they will be able to forge a different future – one coloured by honesty, repentance and generosity; one of which they need not be ashamed. The past is part of them and has shaped their story; it is now part of who they are but it doesn't dictate their future.

In 2009, the band Mumford & Sons recorded a beautiful song called 'Sigh no more' – a phrase that encapsulates concisely what this is all about. The time for shame and regret is moving on into a time of shaping a different future, recognizing the sins of the past but removing their debilitating sting. They – and we – need 'sigh no more' because being embraced by love and mercy transforms the way we look and see and think and live.

Christmas will offer us this freedom in the most unexpected way. God comes among us in the vulnerability of the baby in Bethlehem. The child will grow into the adult whose freedom and shamelessness will offer liberation, forgiveness, healing and hope to those who dare to let go of their pride and guilt and narcissism. Jesus of Nazareth will open the eyes of the blind and unstop the ears of those who for too long have not been able to hear good news of freedom and forgiveness. Not everyone will hear or see this as good news – especially those who have much to lose – and there will be a price to pay; but those who dare to drop their illusions (or who have by virtue of circumstances lost them) will be freed to live a new life, transparent and unafraid.

God of freedom, set us free from our love of guilt and shame, that we might be agents of forgiveness and grace to those among whom we live today. Amen.

WEEK 5: THURSDAY

Steadfast love (54.10)

My steadfast love shall not depart.

I often wonder why the only verses from the Bible that are ever turned into worship songs seem to be the nice ones. We don't seem to sing songs of warning or threat; only songs of hope and promise. What is going on here – especially given that the Psalms cover the whole gamut of human emotion, from joy to bewilderment to grief and unresolved misery?

I guess one reason is that we tend unconsciously to locate ourselves in the biblical narrative in times and places where we feel under pressure or threat (or exile?) and long for deliverance. We want to hear the good news of future blessing rather than hear ourselves being addressed by prophetic warning about our spirituality or ethics. Amos spotted this when he wrote, 'Take away from me the noise of your songs; I will not listen to the melody of your harps' (5.23). Songs that proclaim in our worship the nature of God in a way that exposes our own corruption or denial of that nature in our own common life are damnable and embarrassing. However, Amos goes on, 'But let justice roll down like waters, and righteousness like an ever-flowing stream' (5.24). In other words, the language of our worship should be true to the nature and character of God but also honest about our own consistency or lack of it.

The discrepancy between God and us is hard to hide, but so is the dissonance between our theology and the evidence around us (as we have noted many times). What sense are we to make of 'the stead-fast love of the Lord' not departing when it seems to have actually departed a long time ago? How can the Lord's love be said to be steadfast when our circumstances suggest that it has been defeated or negated? Isn't this just a way of rubbing salt in the wounds of exile and loss?

Well, it might be, but only if your concept of love is weak and sen-timental. The steadfast love of the Lord speaks of a love that is not susceptible to circumstantial change or fluctuation. This love is not deflected by emotion or failure on the part of the loved. Such love does not depend on reciprocation or bargaining, but is rooted in covenant and the character of the Lover. Love like this is not fickle, cannot be bought (or sold) and has to be trusted when things deny its reality.

This sort of love does not just strive to make everything better or to paper over the cracks of failure and denial. God's love is utterly realistic, unafraid of horror and disappointment and remains firm in the face of everything that seeks to undermine it. Rejection does not negate it; manipulation cannot distort it.

This love does not rush to resolution when the only way to allow people to lose their illusions and fantasies is to allow history to take its course. God will not be rushed – which means that exile and loss can also be an expression of the steadfast love of a God who takes people seriously as moral agents whose accountability makes them who they are meant to be. Denial of this accountability and its consequences in fact dehumanizes us by removing from us the accountability that guarantees our moral freedom in the first place. That is why the Old Testament is so full of conditionality: if you don't live correctly, your society will be distorted and you will have to live with the consequences . . . and you will not be spared those.

Here we recall Sheldon Vanauken and the language of living in the light of this love as a 'severe mercy'. God's way is not to coddle us and make us feel nice, but treat us as serious moral players with whom he engages for the good of the world and to whom he commits a ministry of reconciliation.

This might be a trivial example, but I will offer it all the same. I had a massive crisis of faith while living in Germany during my student days and I knew it was crunch time for my being a Christian at all. I longed for a miracle – for God to be real and close – but all I got was silence and absence and a lot of space for doing some serious thinking about God, the world and me. It took more than seven years to build from this a faith that was no longer romantic but inhabited the real world. During this time, I heard the language of God and God's love as a form of mockery at my own disillusionment. It turned out in retrospect to be an example of the mercy of a God whose love was steadfast enough to let me go, make me grow up and compel me to own and be responsible for my Christian discipleship – not because of a nice confirming experience but because of the worked-out conviction that God is there and loves his world, even when he seems absent and silent. God is not a puppet-master.

This is pertinent to the questions we ask as we approach Christmas. Jesus was missed by most people. His entry into a mucky world was hardly explosive, yet quietly and unobtrusively, he changed the way we look at and see and think about and live with the love of a God who takes us seriously and loves us whatever.

Lord, surprise us with your steadfast love, especially on those mornings when the clouds hide the sun and the light is dimmed by the darkness. Amen.

WEEK 5: FRIDAY

No 'ultimate now' (54.11)

O afflicted one, storm-tossed, and not comforted.

The grass really is never greener on the other side, is it? Yet we often speak and behave in such a way as to suggest that if we can only sort today's problem or challenge, then all will be well in the future. Each time I have changed my job or role, I have been glad to let go of a number of seemingly intractable problems (or, if I am honest, people) and move on and start again. Of course, what happens is that five minutes after starting the new role, I realize that I have just taken on a load of new problems (and people). There is no panacea, there is no nirvana.

This is reflected in Isaiah's reference to the 'afflicted one, storm-tossed, and not comforted'. We have been through all the experiences of exile and loss and have begun to wake up to the call of God for the future in which hope will not be disappointed and faith will be built. However, there will still be those among the exiles who are not comforted, for whom the battering has been severe and the wounds deep.

One of U2's most affecting songs declares that they haven't been able to find what they have been searching for. Despite the experiences of life, the searchings and yearnings and longings for hope, there seems to be no escape from the darkness. Does that sound familiar? I remember once being impressed by the bishop who, on entering the church where I served my curacy, saw a huge banner that proclaimed, 'You shall go out with joy!' He asked me, 'What about those who go out as sad or unresolved or as wounded as when they came in? Should they pretend to a joy they do not have or should they give up on a God who promises much but always disappoints?'

The reality of life is such that it just keeps going and we can't always control it. We also lose our sense of perspective by assuming that 'now' is the ultimate – all that matters and the only reality there can be – and 'the what might be' is mere fantasy or wishful imagination. Today is tomorrow's yesterday and so it will carry on for eternity.

The question we might want to address here, however, is not to do with our own longings for resolution or healing, but how we support and love those who are 'storm-tossed' and find no comfort.

The quick answer to the question is that the love and mercy of God will be experienced by most people through the touch and care of the people who bear the name – that is, the character – of the God they claim to serve. In other words, Christians must be the answer to their own prayers for those who suffer or struggle, bringing solace, support and encouragement at the heart of the storm being experienced.

The classic text here is found in the oldest writing of the Old Testament: Job. Apparently blessed by wealth, health and good fortune, Job loses everything he held dear in quick succession and finds himself 'blessed' by the pastoral care of friends. The trouble is, the friends offer little that is helpful. They do, however, stick with him in his suffering and do not hide away because their theology is challenged by reality.

Let's be blunt. We are mortal human beings, living in a contingent world. As the scientist John Polkinghorne wrote in his excellent and accessible book *Quarks, Chaos and Christianity*, we live in a world in which cells multiply; in such a system mutations must be able to occur. That is where cancer comes in. Starkly put, the freedom to live in a physical world comes at the cost of potential aberration, illness and dying (something that came a bit too close to home for me when I had a minor stroke towards the end of 2018). Even if illness is not the problem, but relationships, loneliness or circumstance grind us down, the storm is real and the tossing about in it uncomfortable. This experience, however, is part and parcel of being a human being in the world created as it is by the God who loves us anyway.

So, just as some of Isaiah's exiles will rise to the encouragement of imagining a new world and a return to freedom in their homeland, so will others continue to despair – afflicted, storm-tossed and not comforted. Maybe the best we can do for such people is to continue singing the songs of home, keep the hope vicariously alive – when I can't pray, others do the praying for me – and stay with them even when there is nothing more to say and nothing we can say or do will resolve their predicament.

This is immensely hopeful. God is totally realistic about the human condition and our sensitivity to circumstances and matters beyond our emotional or physical control. This is the reality into which he will plunge himself at Christmas in the cry of a tiny babe.

Lord, who knows what it is to feel abandoned, rejected and alone in the midst of suffering, draw close to us when we are lonely or storm-tossed and spur us on to care in your name for those who suffer. Amen.

WEEK 5: SATURDAY

Choose life (55.3)

Incline your ear, and come to me.

In the end, the exiles will have to decide whether to return to their homeland or stay where they are and with the life they have got used to (and, possibly, benefited from). But choose they must. It is all very well complaining for several generations about all the bad things that have happened or been done to them, but the time comes when they must take responsibility for their own choices and live with the consequences. It is called 'growing up'.

This is the flipside of many stories recounted in the Bible. Abram was called to pack up his family and his things and embark on a journey to an unknown destination: he could have declined. Noah could have said 'no' to building a big boat during very good inland weather. Moses could have continued to resist God's call to stand up to Pharaoh – and who would have blamed him? Jeremiah could have refused to speak truth to power and Ruth could have stayed put in her familiar territory. Zacchaeus could have stayed up his tree, Simon could have opted for his fishing career, Zebedee could have refused to let his sons abandon the family business to go walkabout with the Galilean carpenter-turned-preacher, and the woman who touched the hem of Jesus' cloak could have stayed silent and anonymous. Bartimaeus didn't have to take heart, get up and come to Jesus who was calling him. Paul might have weighed up the cost and decided to be an academic theologian, leaving church planting among the Gentiles to someone else.

Presumably, Jesus could have given in to the temptations in the desert and really could have rejected what was to happen after Gethsemane.

The point is, each of these – and many more besides – had to make a decision, take responsibility and live with the consequences of that commitment. There is no other way and we can't go through life blaming someone else for what happens to us as a result of being human or the choices we have made.

In his powerful and challenging book *Discipleship*, the young German theologian Dietrich Bonhoeffer knocks on the head any concept of what he calls 'cheap grace' and insists that, faced with the challenges of the day – in his case Nazism and the systematic extermination of people – Christians have to make a choice and live with it. In his case, he consented to work for the overthrow of Adolf Hitler and ended up being hanged at Flossenburg on 9 April 1945 – a final act of vindictiveness by the Führer. Having wrestled with his conscience and the ethical questions around killing another person, he made his decision.

Archbishop Oscar Romero was warned many times to stop challenging the military regime, whose behaviour and policies he thought to be godless and inhumane. But he kept on at it – in the name of Christ, not out of some heroic narcissism – to the point where he was shot dead while celebrating mass on 24 March 1980.

Now, most of us do not feel that we face such life-and-death decisions, but we all face choices about whom we will serve. Remember that challenge by Joshua to his recalcitrant people who kept forgetting their own story (24.15):

> Now if you are unwilling to serve the LORD, choose this day whom you will serve, whether the gods your ancestors served in the region beyond the River or the gods of the Amorites in whose land you are living; but as for me and my household, we will serve the LORD.

There is no neutrality here. Not to serve the Lord (Yahweh) is to serve another god. To decline the call of God is to heed the call of another god. A negative choice for one way is, at the same time, a positive choice for another way. So, if we don't choose God's way, then whose way are we choosing at any point?

For the exiles, this was a crunch point. They could blame previous generations for getting them into the mess that led to their exile. They could accuse their ancestors of having forgotten the basic story that gave them identity and purpose as a people. They could accuse the godless foreigners of having victimized and oppressed and exploited them. In the end, however, they have to take responsibility for what they chose to do in shaping their future and creating what, for their grandchildren, would become an inherited world.

Isaiah can represent God's invitation clearly and unambiguously: 'Incline your ear, and come to me'. There can be no compulsion, however . . . and the invitation to commitment can be declined.

This is something that will be worked out by everyone in every generation. Even in the iconic 1996 film *Trainspotting*, the heroin-addicted Renton rants about being told to choose the things most people choose – to get a job, have a family, to live – but he chose something else.

What none of us can do is not choose.

We celebrate Christmas and the birth of the vulnerable baby in the manger, but that baby will grow up and become difficult. He will choose and, in turn, ask others to choose to follow him. It will lead to a cross. As Christmas is about God surprising earth with heaven, however, so will we find that the cross is not the end of the story of God and his people, his commitment to them and their responsive commitment to God.

Lord, incline your ear to us, our longings and our fears and inspire us to come to you in faith, committed to following Jesus wherever he leads and whatever the cost. Amen.

Week 6: Going back a different way

WEEK 6: SUNDAY

Introduction to the week

Advent allows us the space and time to resist the pressure to rush to Christmas so that, when we get there, our minds and spirits are ready for the surprise of Emmanuel, God With Us. It's a sort of delayed gratification, yet it is not simply about individual satisfaction or spiritual fulfilment; Advent allows us the opportunity to rethink and retell the story of God and his people, shining light on both individual piety and the common obligations of God's people in God's (often hostile) world.

The longing of Isaiah's exiles for a resolution of their own estrangement and dislocation has provided for us an imaginative vehicle for reflecting on our own faith, vision, hope and resilience. I can't answer the hard question of how I would have behaved in exile. Would I have been one of those living in the past, wanting to return to some imaginary golden age of home, or one of those looking simply for liberation into a new future? Perhaps I would have been one of those thinking that today is the 'ultimate now' and, therefore, our vocation is simply to make the best of the here and now and not think too much of how things might be shaped in the future (or my responsibility for joining in that shaping). I don't know, but I definitely don't assume that I would have been one of the visionary heroes of the faith.

As we move from Christmas towards Epiphany, we encounter the Magi from the East. These astrologers are looking for Jesus (though they wouldn't have put it like that). In the end, they don't meet the

Messiah in a context of peaceful religiosity; rather, they find themselves the object of political suspicion, scheming and potential violence – unwitting agents of infanticide, unless they have their wits about them in all their conversations. This is the world of Herod, the Romans, cheap human life, power struggles and cruelty.

So as we continue our journey with the exiles towards their new world, we do so in the company of these strange, wise foreigners who find themselves caught up in something far more powerful, dangerous and intriguing than they could ever have imagined. Not surprisingly, they went home from their encounters with Jesus and Herod via a different road. This brings together political canniness, spiritual wisdom, human courage and thoughtful, reactive planning. For them, meeting Jesus did not turn the world into magic.

However, as Rowan Williams warned: 'Looking at Jesus seriously changes things. If we don't want to be changed, it is better not to look too hard.'

WEEK 6: MONDAY

Being found (55.6)

Seek the LORD while he may be found.

In his famous poem 'The Journey of the Magi' (1927, Faber and Gwyer), T. S. Eliot imagines these strange sojourners returning from their discovery of Jesus (and Herod) and being dissatisfied with the old life to which they returned. Their journey and its focus had changed the way they looked at the world and their own purposeful living. It had changed *them*. They were the same, but different; they were now restless as a result of finding the unlikely new king.

More than this, however, they knew that they had found in the birth of the baby an invitation to a death also. Eliot calls this birth and death a 'hard and bitter agony for us'. This journey had given birth within them to a new vision – a new intuition for how life in the world might be in the light of this young king who had surprised them with dissatisfaction. They knew that if new birth was to flourish, old ways must die.

I was once asked in a BBC radio interview what the point of the Church is. I replied (making it up on the spot): the job of the Church is to create the space in which people can find that they have been found by God. This notion has deep biblical roots. Adam and Eve hide from the God who sees through them, but it is God who comes looking for them in the garden in the cool of the day, asking, 'Adam, where are you?' Isaiah's exiles feel abandoned by God for several generations, but it is God who sends the prophets to comfort, challenge and encourage them that he was not finished with them yet. In Jesus of Nazareth, we discover that it is God who comes to us and meets us where we least expect him. In the final vision of a new heaven and a new Earth in Revelation 21, it is heaven that comes down to Earth and not the other way around. We think we find God, but discover the mercy that it is, in fact, God who has already found us . . . and simply invites us to respond in love.

Ben Quash (Professor of Christianity and the Arts at King's College London) has written a fascinating book called *Found Theology* in which he explores and illustrates this theme more boldly. The title itself is evocative. Recognizing that we have been found by God – it is about God, grace, mercy and love – represents the beginning of being a Christian.

This, I suggest, is akin to the experience of Isaiah's exiles, so many centuries before Jesus appeared in Bethlehem, Egypt and Nazareth. They have sought God in the midst of their distress and found only silence; they have looked for signs of their deliverance, only to buckle down to present exilic reality while time and space compel a reimagining of their faith. What they begin to discern in the end is the haunting whisper of hope that their end is not nigh, even if the end of their exile is. They too are discovering, slowly and painfully, that they too have been found and not forgotten by God.

One of the most vivid biblical illustrations of this comes in the parable of the Prodigal Son – or should that be the parable of the Waiting Father (as the German theologian Helmut Thielicke put it) or even the parable of the Elder Brother? We can take our pick, but our choice will illumine what we think Jesus was getting at. Whatever, it is clear that the father in the story has not only been waiting and hoping for his son's return but also looking for it. He would not have seen his scheming son in the far distance had he not been watching. He then runs out to meet him and embarrasses him (and the rest of the family, no doubt) by welcoming and celebrating the unlikely return. The son calculates for revenge, but meets wild generosity; he expects little, but finds himself wanted, loved and restored.

Of course, our usual experience is that we look for God in the usual places and discover that, in fact, he finds us in surprising ways. The slave trader John Newton wrote his famous hymn 'Amazing Grace' to express the experience of having 'now been found' – and then found that his life had to change in the light of who had found him.

The exiles will one day go home, but home will have changed and moved on; and they will go home different in the light of their experience of exile and the apparent absence of God. They will go home a different way – and different as a people. The Magi find, according to Eliot, that they cannot simply go back to how things were before their journey. I suspect we will find the same. Any encounter with the surprising Jesus will change us and, through us, potentially change the world around us. We seek the Lord – with our imagination, intellect, body, soul and mind – while he may be found, but we then discover that we have already been found. That changes everything.

God, who causes us to search for meaning and truth, open our eyes and our hearts to your searching gaze, that we might find our home in you and know that you have already found us. Amen.

WEEK 6: TUESDAY

Under the mercy (55.7)

For he will abundantly pardon.

Why is forgiveness so difficult? Not the forgiving, but the being forgiven?

Go back again to the parable of the Prodigal Son, Waiting Father, Elder Brother and imagine the experience. Understandably, this story has often been used to illustrate the experience of God's grace following repentance and conversion, but the actual story suggests a more complicated experience. The prodigal son doesn't 'repent'; he schemes and calculates. Being at his lowest point, he works out that even as a servant on his father's estate, he would at least have food and lodging. He would manipulate his father's generosity and their blood relationship in order to improve his own lot.

Now imagine, having worked out his story, he comes back home only to find himself welcomed, surprised by joy and restored into the family, despite the reservations of his elder brother. Such extravagant joy at his return would have completely undermined any calculation or scheme . . . or even genuine repentance and sorrow. There is always something in us as human beings that thinks we should pay the price for our freedom and, by repaying the debt (however interpreted), we earn our place and restore our pride. Not so here, when such calculation is ridden over and embarrassed by grace.

For the exiles of the sixth century before Jesus, this experience would have been no easier to comprehend. Their exile, as they have repeatedly been reminded, was the result of their losing sight of God, his character and his call on their lives. Now it is to come gradually to an end, facing them as a people with a new set of considerations and choices as they prepare for a new future. At the heart of the new challenge will be this: that if they have received the generosity, forgiveness and grace of God, then they too must offer – live out, whatever the cost – that same generosity and grace among those whose lives or land they share. If God will 'abundantly pardon', then this must be what will characterize those who bear God's name.

This contingency runs like a thread through the Scriptures. Consider again the Lord's Prayer – the prayer Jesus taught his friends: 'Forgive us our sins as we forgive those who sin against us.' You can't separate one from the other. We cannot proclaim a forgiving God if we – as Church, congregation or individual Christian – do not forgive those who injure or offend us. The Beatitudes link being blessed with the blessing of others by the life lived.

For Isaiah's exiles, the precondition for this freedom is the recognition that there is something to be pardoned in the first place. Maybe this is the hardest bit for societies, churches or individuals: admitting the need, acknowledging that I cannot save/heal myself. As we have seen in a previous week, go back to that very early Hebrew creed in Deuteronomy 26 and then on to the later warnings about how the people should behave when they entered the land of promise. Remember that their rituals were intended to remind them (literally re-mind, keep bringing their mind and will in line with their memory and vocation) that they had once been refugees with nothing to their name, dependent on the generosity of foreigners. Forget this and they forget their controlling narrative and lose their vocation to be people who resemble in their common life and social order the character of the God whose name they claim. It then won't be long before they are treating other refugees, poor and hungry people, as their slaves. Being a servant will have mutated into being served – something about which Jesus had something to say later on.

As, millennia later and in a different time and culture, we proceed from Christmas to Epiphany, we face a similar question and challenge. If we have found forgiveness and freedom in Jesus Christ, then how are we living it out in our own relationships, our shaping of local and national social order, our politics? Do we journey with some vague sense of need to a place where we meet Emmanuel, only to walk away because he isn't the sort of Emmanuel we hoped to find?

Some people have suggested that this is too easy. We can sin our boots off . . . and then do a bit of confession or sorry-saying and be forgiven; suddenly everything is better and we can draw a line under the offence and be free. Well, yes, to a point, but that only makes sense if we leave out of the equation any notion of what we have described above: living now in the light of the forgiveness received and, therefore, paying the price of justice, love and reconciliation. In other words, it doesn't stop at having been pardoned. What happens to the forgiven individual must have social consequences because we are relational beings whose lives cannot be lived in silos.

The liberation of pardon changes the world and sets the offender free. However, this is not just freedom *from*, it is freedom *for*. The two cannot be separated.

God of the future, remind us to remember our past and the story of your people through the ages, that we might always know our need and our obligations to those among whom we live. Amen.

WEEK 6: WEDNESDAY

Always learning (55.8)

My thoughts are not your thoughts.

When under pressure or feeling sorry for myself, my eyes go down and the world shrinks. It is at times like this that I need to wake up and remember the world is bigger than my little circle of life.

We touched on this when we took a brief look at Cain and the city he built and called Enoch (Genesis 4). In a featureless expanse of desert, we construct a settlement within defensive walls and this lo-cus gives us a sense of place and meaning. Jacques Ellul suggests that this is what human beings do, metaphorically: we build a small uni-verse of meaning because we can't live without knowing who we are and where we belong. It is the penetration of the defensive wall that opens a breach and challenges or invites us to look outside the walls to a bigger world.

The great Canadian singer-songwriter Bruce Cockburn has a bril-liant album from 1998 called *Big Circumstance* on which he plays around with the idea that, as our circumstances draw our attention down and inwards to ourselves, we can't escape from the attention of God – Big Circumstance – beyond us. In the song 'Shipwrecked at the stable door', he refers several times to the album's title and, in doing so, he de-romanticizes any sweet or easy notions of provi-dence, personal security or tidiness. Big Circumstance can't be con-trolled by us and can't be bought, and we all end up in a tomb.

This notion of the 'Big Circumstance' gives us a sideways angle on understanding what is meant by Isaiah when the differences and distinctions between human beings and God are mentioned: 'For my thoughts are not your thoughts, nor are your ways my ways, says the LORD. For as the heavens are higher than the earth, so are my ways higher than your ways and my thoughts than your thoughts' (55.8–9).

In Cockburn's terms, the exiles in Babylon are being confronted with a choice here. Some of them hear God's invitation to shape a future back home, but they are too rooted in the familiarity of the alien empire to contemplate a further uprooting and moving on. They would prefer the limitations and offerings of Babylon than to assume responsibility for taking heart, getting up and responding deliberately to the call of God (as Bartimaeus heard it from Jesus' friends in Mark 10). The offer of newness implies the need for growth and development, which, in turn, come at cost: something is always lost when we decline the comfort of sclerosis and security.

There is a further warning in these verses. The reflex to have God endorse your own politics or preferences must be avoided. God's perspective is longer and broader and deeper and higher than any limited human capacity to understand or imagine. Wrapped up in my own little world, I can easily miss out on how the bigger and wider world might be reshaped; and if I simply shape God in my own image, miraculously finding that his view is my view and his ways coincide with my ways, then trouble lies ahead.

If God coming among us happened in a surprising way and if the Servant of Isaiah appears a little disappointing in terms of power and glory (or 'winning', as Donald Trump might put it), then it must be clear that my thoughts need to be subjected to God's thoughts and my ways to his ways. People like the Prodigal Son think they can buy God off, but discover when face to face with him that outrageous generosity has no place for such feeble calculation. Discerning the thoughts and ways of God demands humble attention to God in prayer and listening to the world around us; it then means testing our conclusions against the narrative of Scripture in the light of the Church's experience through the ages.

Simply to assume that God thinks the way I do, shares the same political inclinations or convictions I have or prioritizes 'issues' over people (against the drift of Scripture) is to misunderstand what it is to be a disciple, a learner and a follower of the man from Galilee. Fundamental to following Jesus is a willingness to change my mind – to repent and look, see, think and live differently. To behave otherwise is to completely miss the point.

History is littered with examples of Christians hitching their theological wagon to a spirit of the current imperial age. Hitler got his 'German Christians' to back his authoritarian regime on the grounds, partly, that he was bringing order out of chaos – a strong biblical theme. Dietrich Bonhoeffer went to his death on the gallows because he saw through this and, with friends in the Confessing Church, refused to bow down to the new idols (that are never so new after all – which is why we read history). Karl Barth lost his professorial chair in Bonn and moved to Basel because he could not be seduced or intimidated by the Reich (literally, the Empire). Others chose differently and retained their status, but lost something along the way.

Most of us do not face such stark dilemmas (yet), but all of us face the small dilemmas that, if we duck the call to obedience to God's ways, we gradually smooth the way to compromise and exile. We do this when, for example, we don't challenge the normalization of lying, misrepresentation and intimidation in our political life – or when we meekly accept corruption or short-sighted decision-making that reinforces security for rich people at the expense of poor people.

Whose thoughts do mine reflect?

God, whose thoughts and ways sometimes seem unfathomable, clear the fog of confusion and help us to see more clearly what it might be to reflect your image in your world – whatever the cost. Amen.

WEEK 6: THURSDAY

My word (55.11)

My word . . . shall not return to me empty.

The prophecy to the exiles is now coming to a conclusion. They have heard words of criticism, comfort, challenge and encouragement, promise and threat, but why should they believe any of it? God, their God, has been silent and their lot at the hands of the Babylonian empire has not been good. They have tried to hang on to their story and identity – to keep alive the language and songs of home while living in a strange land.

Isaiah takes them back to their core theology. Strip away all the distractions and what are you left with?

Isaiah understands that, before the exiles can make their decision regarding a return to their homeland, they need to go back to basics. The basics for them take them back to the creation narratives, which, in their Genesis forms, were probably written during exile anyway. Reread Genesis 1—2 and what comes over loud and clear is this: God in creation brings order out of chaos. When we feel abandoned or distressed, look at the world around – the rain and the sun, the vegetation and the life – and remember the story that sees everything around you as owing its existence to God the Creator. 'In the beginning God . . .' (Genesis 1.1, NIV) and at the end of our imagination or distress, God. He who was faithful in creation is faithful now and will be faithful in the unknown and uncertain future.

Now, the exiles are not the only people who need to be recalled to what fundamentally matters. When I drive up into the Yorkshire Dales or look down from an aircraft at the Earth 13,000 metres beneath me, I feel humbled. After all, I could die now and all this will just carry on. The mountains and hills, the cycle of sun and rain, the seasons of the year, the flowing of the rivers and the tides that drive the oceans – they won't notice my absence. I am a blip in the history of the multiverses and nature doesn't care very much whether the carbon of my body is carried in flesh and blood or in some other form. This, I suggest, is both humbling and utterly liberating. It reinforces the invitation to put our faith, trust and hope in God the Creator and not in some finite formula for ensuring my well-being.

I realize that not everybody will want to think this way, but it is certainly how the early Christians thought of it. Their identity was primarily in Christ and everything else flowed from that. Just read the letters of Paul in the New Testament and this comes over loud and clear.

However, Isaiah also evokes echoes of another element in the creation narratives that form the foundation of his people's self-understanding. In Genesis, the cosmos comes into being by means of words – words uttered by God. The words are creative and generative: 'Let there be . . .'. Theologians have written copious volumes trying to dig out the depths of meaning in these simple words and the simple way in which they are framed as the order of creation is drawn out of the chaos and void. 'Let there be.'

This, of course, points to the nature of God as consistent and fruitful. God's writ runs in the real world of flesh and blood, rock and water. As rain and snow enable the Earth to be watered and life in all its cycles to be fertile, so will God's 'let there be' produce consequences that shape the real world. As the Earth is nourished by the elements, so will God nourish the people who hear and respond to his 'let there be'. God's words of promise to the exiles are not empty; they will change things just as the rain and snow shape our natural world.

The exiles are just like any of us in the twenty-first century Western world. At times of emptiness or distress, when our reference points have disappeared and we fear the chaotic power of forces around us over which we seem to have little control, we also long to detect the whisper of hope and order. We long to believe that what feels like 'the end' might be nudged by the faint solidity of a 'let there be' – the promise of a future that is open to life and nurture and flourishing and fulfilment.

That is what Isaiah is holding before the eyes and memory of his exiled people. The end is not the end. Dare to believe that, like the Magi searching for their strange king, we are not condemned to re-tread the same old paths but can go back by a different route and find ourselves breathing a fresh air in a new place of possibility. God's word will not evaporate into nothingness; God's 'let there be' will always find a way to create newness after loss.

Lord, whose word is faithful and fruitful, speak to us and root within us that hope which, fed by your promises, emanates into lives and words, bringing hope to others. Amen.

WEEK 6: FRIDAY

Joy and peace (55.12)

You shall go out in joy, and be led back in peace.

I have just discovered that 'Joy and Peace' is a brand of women's shoes – 'an emblem of quality European footwear, serving our prestigious ladies with fine Italian footwear craftsmanship', as the company's website puts it. Marvellous. I am left wondering if the right foot is peace and the left joy or vice versa.

Nobody has a monopoly on joy and peace, after all. Some people I know sign off their emails and letters with such a wish. Many religions and philosophies promise to reward their followers with these wonderful experiences. Nowadays, advertisers even promise us that if we wear particular clothes, drive particular cars, watch particular sports or eat particular foods, we will experience joy and peace (among other excitements). Naturally, these are always hinted at and never defined. Joy and peace.

Isaiah wasn't encumbered by modern technologies or consumer capitalism, nor was he stupid enough to think that people in exile would be easily conned into some future-orientated wishful thinking based on a slogan. His people had 'done' idols and fantasies and found their human disorientation and sense of existential (as well as actual physical) displacement could not be resolved that easily. So, when he concludes his address to those in exile, promising a future for them, he needs more than shallow seduction. He takes them back to their story and the God who has called them consistently from the beginning.

To speak of 'going out' will immediately evoke association with and memory of the exodus. The people of God, trapped in miserable oppression at the hands of a foreign empire, discover that they are helpless to liberate themselves. Then, in an event that comes to form the dominant episode for their understanding of God and themselves as a people, they are led out of Egypt towards a land of promise. Here too God will not be rushed – a generation has to die before they can truly be said to have left Egypt behind and be ready for a new life in the new world. Forty years in the desert learning to let go of the past and look to a different future – still trusting in the God who has created, called, rescued and restored them throughout.

'You shall go out in joy' is the song that will burst from the people as they discover that God's promised liberation from exile is no fantasy and no joke. They shall experience this new exodus as a reflection of the original one and, to use the words of the psalmist, their mourning (of loss) will be turned into dancing (see Psalm 30.11) as they slowly walk towards their new future. The God of the exodus is demonstrating that he has not gone away, has not changed and has remained faithful to his own character and purposes in his world.

Yet joy is accompanied by peace. Not the absence of conflict or problem or challenge. Not the imaginary fluffiness of some other-worldly contentment, undisturbed by other people or some other inconvenience. Rather, peace seeps through, based on a deep and long memory of God's faithfulness. When Isaiah speaks of peace, he is rooted in the realities of this world, speaking the words of a God who is not remote from the real world but utterly committed to it.

Peace doesn't always get a good or helpful press. The sharing of 'the Peace' in churches during the Holy Communion service sometimes becomes a bit of a friendly free-for-all (unless you are a newcomer, easily embarrassed or trying to concentrate on the holy mysteries), when its origin and purpose lay elsewhere. The early Christians would listen to the reading and exposition of Scripture – God's word – and bring their prayers to God before moving into the meal that memorializes the self-sacrifice of Jesus and his injunction that his friends should emulate (embody, even) him. Before they could proceed to the breaking of bread, however, the unbaptized would leave, the doors would be shut and the baptized would have to put right what was wrong between them. Not a quick handshake, but the full reconciliation works. It was serious, costly and world-changing. Try that next Sunday.

Isaiah's exiles will return to their homeland with the command to live peacefully, to enflesh the peace that characterizes the God they serve. This means not running away from the challenges of peace-making among themselves and others. Peace assumes relationship. It assumes the absence of peace where reconciliation is avoided and being right is prioritized and valued over being right with others.

Joy and peace, exodus and return. Change and transformation as God's people grapple together with the challenge of being like the God who has created, called, shaped, forgiven and renewed them. This is the promise to the exiles: you shall exodus in joy and you shall return (be led – again, you need a saviour) in peace . . . and this will only be the beginning of a new journey, a new life, in a place that is both familiar and yet different. God is faithful; will you be faithful to his call?

Lord of exodus and return, of joy and peace, lead all your people in the ways of justice and love, that peace may reign and joy burst from our hearts. Amen.

WEEK 6: SATURDAY

Creation renewed (55.12)

The trees of the field shall clap their hands.

How we read the Bible matters enormously.

I remember being at a radio studio with a group of agnostic and atheist scientists, writers, actors and musicians. We had been talking about the possibility of being both a scientist and a theist. Inevitably, the scientific reliability of Genesis came up as if it was a knock-down intellectual argument against the possibility of God. My job was to do some literacy thinking. I said something like this: when we read in Isaiah that 'the trees of the field will clap their hands', we don't point out of the window and scream something about 'Trees don't have hands, so this is rubbish!' Rather, we know that we are reading poetry. However, if I read about trees clapping hands in a scientific textbook, I would be worried. It is important to know what sort of literature we are reading. Genesis 1—11 is poetry interested in the 'why' of life, not a book of chemistry, biology or physics exploring the mechanics of creation – the 'how' questions.

So here Isaiah concludes his writing to those in exile and awaiting return to their homeland with words of exuberant promise: joy, peace, trees clapping their hands and the world being reordered. You can see why. The creation narratives proclaim that the God of the cosmos brought order out of chaos, loved what he had made and has never changed his mind since. The exodus demonstrates in real time and space that God is on the side of justice and liberation, that he sees and creates a future when no one else can spot anything other than endless misery, a world closing down. In Isaiah and the prophets, God warns his people to remember their God and their story or risk losing their way – then accompanies them through the consequences of living in a disorderly way to the point when they can discern a more faithful future.

As we move on from the prophets, we will meet those whose lives have closed down but who find in Emmanuel a new hope and a future that they thought was closed to them for ever. There is genuine celebration among those who are surprised by joy and peace, even if those professionally committed to a theology of the same actually miss the point when confronted by it. (Remember the Pharisees who, on seeing a woman healed after two decades of infirmity and ostracism, can only complain that Jesus should have waited until a weekday to do it as doing it on the sabbath was not allowed?)

However, Isaiah also wants his hearers to expand their vision of God and his purposes beyond the navel-gazing limitations of their own little experience. By invoking rain and snow and trees with hands, he is asking his people to open their eyes to a bigger vision. God is not a tribal deity in competition with other tribal deities to see who is the most powerful in defence of the tribe. God is not 'their' God – some sort of a commodity or possession that marks them out from other communities or people. God is not located just in the present, but constantly reminds his people of the stories of the past that shape their understanding and experience of themselves and the world. This God is the Creator, Sustainer, Redeemer and Lover of the cosmos – not just of human beings, but human beings as part of the created order.

Perhaps this brings twenty-first-century Christians to a challenge that will shape whether or not we are faithful to the God who calls us. Faced with all we know of the complex enormity of the universes and the place of this tiny planet in it, and confronted daily by the cries of the planet against its ruthless exploitation by rapacious powers of consumption, is now not the time for God's people to hear God's reminder that the future might need to look different? As the exiles will return to a home that has changed and now demands a different way of living, so Christians cannot avoid the challenge to resist the demands and hegemonies of exploitative industries that provide material wealth at the expense of the world we say is God's . . . and of people whose lives are destroyed by the greed, selfishness and violence of the powerful.

The trees of the field will clap their hands as a humble people remember their story and return a different way. However, denial of God's way might mean that one day the trees will have no hands to clap. Then the old warnings will need to be heard again. So will the old promise that our end can always be God's new beginning.

Lord of creation and Lover of all, forgive us our shortened sight, our narrowness of mind and our deafness to the cries of the earth. Set our hearts and minds free to hear your call to a different way and give us the courage to follow you in it. Amen.

Questions

Week 1: Hearing voices

- Do you think that Christians are living in exile today? If so, what does this mean for the task of the Church?
- How are your imagination, heart and mind being 'grasped by hope'? Are they strong enough to withstand exile?
- If exile is an appropriate image to use here, what might it mean for us to learn to wait for God together? How might this shape our worship, our prayers and our reading of the Bible?
- How do we ensure that we're not just making God in our own image, hearing the words we want to hear? Are we open/brave enough to get our blind spots checked out? How might we best do that?
- Have you discovered any flowers in your desert that you would never have seen had you run away from the hard times?

Week 2: Easy idols

- What are the idols that distract me and offer a cheap imitation of the Creator?
- What are the implications of being a member of a group (the Church) that knows itself to be chosen by God? How do we know we are 'chosen'?
- What would our common life look like if we were to reflect the character of the God who lays down his life for us?
- How might we avoid the pitfalls of echo-chambers in which we hear what we want to hear and screen out what might be the voice of God? What implications might my answer have for my social media use or sources of news consumption?

- Are your ears open to the call of God to be a shaper of the future and builder of God's kingdom here, where you are? What might this look like to those who look at you/us?

Week 3: Fear and faith

- What are the things that make us fear? How do we hear the call to 'not be afraid'?
- Names change as we encounter God and his call. How does your 'name' speak of the potential God sees in you?
- What can you say to someone who, despite prayer and faithfulness, continues to suffer and finds no relief or healing?
- What 'comfort' might God be calling you away from? Has your suffering become such a part of your identity that you can't let it go?
- How might you formulate – in words they'll understand in the pub – the story of God's faithfulness to you and your response?

Week 4: Power and faithfulness

- What does Jesus 'look like' to you? Would we recognize him or are we too readily impressed by wealth, status or celebrity?
- Where, in the biblical narrative, should we locate the Church today? For example, is this a period when God is silent (1 Samuel 3.1)?
- Is God heard and seen in cultures where secular cynicism doesn't dominate – or where Christians are persecuted on account of their faith?
- What does it mean for you/us to bear the name of God and reflect God's character to the world around us?
- What might it look like for me/us to be agents of light for people who are anguished?

Week 5: Joy will find a way

- Can you recall any times when, despite your experience, joy found a way and the light crept in through the cracks?
- Can you sing Mary's song or which song characterizes what you think about God, the world and yourself?
- What difference does the intrusion of Jesus into the world make when you feel storm-tossed and not comforted?
- What are the potential and actual consequences of choosing to follow Jesus in the twenty-first century?

Week 6: Going back a different way

- Do you have any experience of having been found by God? What difference did and does this make to your way of seeing and being?
- Conscious of living 'under the mercy' of God, how does this make you merciful to others – especially to those you feel don't deserve it?
- What does God's faithfulness to you and your community look like, especially when seen against the long backdrop of God's faithfulness to his people in Isaiah?
- In what ways can your church help you and other Christians to learn how to align your thoughts and perceptions to those of God? How might study of the Bible help you in this and what help might you need to do this effectively?
- Is your passion for God worked out in passion for his world – in creation, politics, economics and our common life? When our local community comes across us, do those within it experience anything of the God of Isaiah?

Bibliography

Baines, Nick, *Hungry for Hope?* (Wells: St Andrew's Press, 2007).

Bell, John, 'God's Surprise', in *Wild Goose Songs: Vol. 1* (Glasgow: Wild Goose Publications, 1987).

Bonhoeffer, Dietrich, *Discipleship* (Minneapolis, MN: Fortress Press, 2015).

Brueggemann, Walter, *Cadences of Home: Preaching among exiles* (Westminster: John Knox Press, 1997).

Brueggemann, Walter, *Redescribing Reality: What we do when we read the Bible* (London: SCM Press, 2009).

Dostoyevsky, Fyodor, *Brothers Karamazov* (London: Penguin, 2003).

Ellul, Jacques, *The Meaning of the City* (Grand Rapids, MI: William B. Eerdmans, 1970).

Gooder, Paula, *The Meaning is in the Waiting* (Norwich: Canterbury Press, 2008).

Koyama, Kosuke, *Three Mile an Hour God* (London: SCM Press, 1979).

Lewis, C. S., *Surprised by Joy* (London: Fontana, 1972).

Martin, Harold Victor, *Kierkegaard, the Melancholy Dane* (London: Epworth Press, 1950).

Mochulsky, Koustantin, *Dostoevsky: His life and work*, translated by Michael A. Minihan (Princeton, NJ: Princeton University Press, 1971).

Polkinghorne, John, *Quarks, Chaos and Christianity* (London: SPCK, 2005).

Pratchett, Terry, *Small Gods* (London: Corgi, 2013).

Quash, Ben, *Found Theology* (London: Bloomsbury, 2013).

Rohr, Richard, *Radical Grace: Daily meditations* (Cincinnati, OH: St Anthony Messenger Press, 1995).

Thielicke, Helmut, *Christ and the Meaning of Life* (Cambridge: James Clarke & Company, 1965).

Thomas, R. S., 'Kneeling', in *Not that He Brought Flowers* (London: Hart-Davis, 1968).

Vanauken, Sheldon, *A Severe Mercy* (London: Hodder & Stoughton, 1977).

Vanauken, Sheldon, *Under the Mercy* (London: Hodder & Stoughton, 1985).

Wallis, Jim, *The Call to Conversion* (Oxford: Monarch, 2006).

Williams, Rowan, *Being Disciples* (London: SPCK, 2016).